SEVEN WIVES AND SEVEN PRISONS

OR EXPERIENCES IN THE LIFE OF A
MATRIMONIAL MANIAC. A TRUE STORY.

L. A. Abbott

Seven Wives and Seven Prisons

L. A. Abbott

© 1st World Library – Literary Society, 2004
PO Box 2211
Fairfield, IA 52556
www.1stworldlibrary.org
First Edition

LCCN: 2004195333

Softcover ISBN: 1-4218-0164-7
Hardcover ISBN: 1-4218-0064-0
eBook ISBN: 1-4218-0264-3

Purchase *"Seven Wives and Seven Prisons"*
as a traditional bound book at:
www.1stWorldLibrary.org/purchase.asp?ISBN=1-4218-0164-7

1st World Library Literary Society is a nonprofit
organization dedicated to promoting literacy by:

- Creating a free internet library accessible from any computer worldwide.
- Hosting writing competitions and offering book publishing scholarships.

Seven Wives and Seven Prisons
contributed by Tim, Ed & Rodney
in support of
1st World Library Literary Society

CONTENTS

CHAPTER I.

THE FIRST AND WORST WIFE

My Early History - THE FIRST MARRIAGE - LEAVING HOME TO PROSPECT - SENDING FOR MY WIFE - HER MYSTERIOUS JOURNEY - WHERE I FOUND HER - TEN DOLLARS FOR NOTHING - A FASCINATING HOTEL CLERK - MY WIFE'S CONFESSION - FROM BAD TO WORSE - FINAL SEPARATION - TRIAL FOR FORGERY - A PRIVATE MARRIAGE - SUMMARY SEPARATION.

SOME one has said that if any man would faithfully write his autobiography, giving truly his own history and experiences, the ills and joys, the haps and mishaps that had fallen to his lot, he could not fail to make an interesting story; and Disraeli makes Sidonia say that there is romance in every life. How much romance, as well as sad reality, there is in the life of a man who, among other experiences, has married seven wives, and has been seven times in prison-solely on account of the seven wives, may be learned from the pages that follow.

I was born in the town of Chatham, Columbia County, New York, in September, 1813. My father was a New Englander, who married three times, and I was the eldest son of his third wife, a woman of Dutch descent, or, as she would have boosted if she had been rich, one of the old Knickerbockers of New York. My parents were simply honest, hard-working, worthy people, who earned a good livelihood, brought up their children to work, behaved themselves, and were respected by their neighbors. They had a homestead and a small farm of thirty acres, and on the place was a blacksmith shop in which my father worked daily, shoeing horses and cattle for farmers and others who came to the shop from miles around.

There were three young boys of us at home, and we had a chance to go to school in the winter, while during the summer we worked on the little farm and did the "chores" about the house and barn. But by the time I was twelve years old I began to blow and strike in the blacksmith shop, and when I was sixteen years old I could shoe horses well, and considered myself master of the trade. At the age of eighteen, I went into business with my father, and as I was now entitled to a share of the profits, I married the daughter of a well-to-do neighboring farmer, and we began our new life in part of my father's house, setting up for ourselves, and doing our own house-keeping.

I ought to have known then that marrying thus early in life, and especially marrying the woman I did, was about the most foolish thing I could do. I found it out afterwards, and was frequently and painfully reminded of it through many long years. But all seemed bright enough at the start. My wife was a good-looking woman of just my own age; her family was most respectable; two of her brothers subsequently became ministers of the gospel; and all the children had been carefully brought up. I was thought to have made a good match; but a few years developed that had wedded a most unworthy woman.

Seventeen months after our marriage, our oldest child, Henry, was born. Meanwhile we had gone to Sidney, Delaware County, where my father opened a shop. I still continued in business with him, and during our stay at Sidney, my daughter, Elizabeth, was born. From Sidney, my father wanted to go to Bainbridge, Chenango, County, N. Y., and I went with him, leaving my wife and the children at Sidney, while we prospected. As usual my father started a blacksmith-shop; but I bought a hundred acres of timber land, went to lumbering, and made money. We had a house about four miles from the village, I living with my father, and as soon as found out that we were doing well in business, I sent to Sidney for my wife and children. They were to come by stage, and were due, after passing through Bainbridge, at our house at four o'clock in the morning. We were up early to meet the stage; but when it arrived, the driver told us that my wife had stopped at the public house in Bainbridge.

Wondering what this could mean, I at once set out with my brother and walked over to the village. It was daylight when we arrived, and knocked loudly at the public house door. After considerable delay, the clerk came to the door and let us in. He also asked as to "take something," which we did. The clerk knew us well, and I inquired if my wife was in the house; he said she was, told us what room she was in, and we went up stairs and found her in bed with her children. Waking her, I asked her why she did not come home, in the stage? She replied that the clerk down stairs told her that the stage did not go beyond the house, and that she expected to walk over, as soon as it was daylight, or that possibly we might come for her.

I declare, I was so young and unsophisticated that I

suspected nothing, and blamed only the stupidity, as I supposed, of the clerk in telling her that the stage did not go beyond Bainbridge. My wife got up and dressed herself and the children, and then as it was broad daylight, after endeavoring, ineffectually, to get a conveyance, we started for home on foot, she leading the little boy, and I carrying the youngest child. We were not far on our way when she suddenly stopped, stooped down, and exclaimed:

"O! see what I have found in the road"-

And she showed me a ten dollar bill. I was quite surprised, and verdantly enough, advised looking around for more money, which my wife, brother and I industriously did for some minutes. It was full four weeks before I found out where that ten dollar bill came from. Meanwhile, my wife was received and was living in her new home, being treated with great kindness by all of us. It was evident, however, that she had something on her mind which troubled her, and one morning, about a month after her arrival, I found her in tears. I asked her what was the matter? She said that she had been deceiving me; that she did not pick up the ten dollar bill in the road; but that it was given to her by the clerk in the public house in Bainbridge; only, however, for this: he had grossly insulted her; she had resented it, and he had given her the money, partly as a reparation, and partly to prevent her from speaking of the insult to me or to others.

But by this time my hitherto blinded eyes were opened, and I charged her with being false to me. She protested she had not been; but finally confessed that she had been too intimate with the clerk at the hotel. I began a suit at law against the clerk; but finally, on account of my wife's family and for the sake of my children, I stopped proceedings, the clerk paying the costs of the suit as far as it had gone, and giving me what I should probably have got from him in the way of damages. My wife too, was apparently so penitent, and I was so much infatuated with her, that I forgave her, and even consented to continue to live with her. But I removed to Greenville, Greene County, N. Y., where I went into the black-smithing business, and was very successful. We lived here long enough to add two children to our little family; but as time went on, the woman became bad again, and displayed the worst depravity. I could no longer live with her, and we finally mutually agreed upon a life-long separation - she insisting upon keeping the children, and going to Rochester where she subsequently developed the full extent of her character.

This, as nearly as I remember, was in the year 1838, and with this came a new trouble upon me. Just before the separation, I received from my brother's wife a note for one hundred dollars, and sold it. It proved to be a forgery. I was temporarily in Troy, N. Y., when the discovery was made, and as I made no secret of my whereabouts at any time, I was followed to Troy, was there arrested, and after lying in jail at Albany one night, was taken next morning to Coxsackie, Greene County, and front thence to Catskill. After one day in jail there, I was brought before a justice and examined on the charge of uttering a forged note. There was a most exciting trial of four days duration. I had two good lawyers who did their best to show that I did not know the note to be forged when I sold it, but the justice seemed determined to bind me over for trial, and he did so, putting me under five hundred dollars' bonds. My half-sister at Sidney was sent for, came to Catskill, and became bail for me. I was released, and my lawyers advised me to leave, which I did at once, and went to Pittsfield, and from there to Worthington, Mass., where I had another half-sister, who was married to Mr. Josiah Bartlett, and was well off.

Here I settled down, for all that I knew to the contrary, for life. For some years past, I had devoted my leisure hours from the forge to the honest endeavor to make up for the deficiencies in my youthful education, and had acquired, among other things, a good knowledge of medicine. I did not however, believe in any of the "schools" particularly those schools that make use of mineral medicines in their practice. I favored purely vegetable remedies, and had been very successful in administering them. So I began life anew, in Worthington, as a Doctor, and aided by my half-sister and her friends, I soon secured a remunerative practice.

I was beginning to be truly happy. I supposed that the final separation, mutually agreed upon between my wife and myself, was as effectual as all the courts in the country could make it, and I looked upon myself as a free man. Accordingly, after I had been in Worthington some months I began to pay attentions to the daughter of a flourishing farmer. She was a fine girl; she received my addresses favorably, and we were finally privately married. This was the beginning of my life-long troubles. In a few weeks her father found out that I had been previously married, and was not, so far as he knew, either a divorced man or a widower. And so it happened, that one day when I was at his house, and with his daughter, he suddenly came home with a posse of people and a warrant for my arrest. I was taken before a justice, and while we were waiting for proceedings to begin, or, possibly for the justice to arrive, I took the excited father aside and said:

"You know I have a fine horse and buggy at the door. Get in with me, and ride down home. I will see your daughter and make everything right with her, and if you will let me run away, I'll give her her the horse and buggy."

The offer was too tempting to be refused. The father had the warrant in his pocket, and he accepted my proposal. We rode to his house, and he went into the back-room by direction of his daughter while she and I talked in the hall. I explained mat- ters as well as I could; I promised to see her again, and that very soon. My horse and buggy were at the door. Hastily bidding my new and young wife "good-bye," I sprang into the buggy and drove rapidly away. The father rushed to the door and raised a great hue and cry, and what was more, raised the neighbors; I had not driven five miles before all Worthington was after me. But I had the start, the best horse, and I led in the race. I drove to Hancock, N.Y., where my pursuers lost the trail; thence to Bennington, Vt., next to Brattleboro, Vt., and from there to Templeton, Mass. What befel me at Templeton, shall be related in the next chapter.

CHAPTER II.

MISERIES FROM MY SECOND MARRIAGE.

LOVE-MAKING IN MASSACHUSETTS - ARREST FOR BIGAMY - TRIAL AT NORTHAMPTON - A STUNNING SENTENCE - SENT TO STATE PRISON - LEARNING THE BRUSH BUSINESS - SHARPENING PICKS - PRISON FARE - IN THE HOSPITAL - KIND TREATMENT - SUCCESSFUL HORSE SHOEING - THE WARDEN MY FRIEND - EFFORTS FOR MY RELEASE - A FULL PARDON.

At Templeton I speedily made known my profession, and soon had a very good medical practice which one or two "remarkable cures" materially increased. I was doing well and making money. I boarded in a respectable farmer's family, and after living there about six months there came another most unhappy occurrence. From the day, almost, when I began to board with this farmer there sprung up a strong attachment between myself and his youngest daughter which soon ripened into mutual love. She rode about with me when I went to see my patients, who were getting to be numerous, and we were much in each other's company.

On one occasion she accompanied me to Worcester where I had some patients. We went to a public house where she and her family were well known, and when she was asked by the landlord how she happened to come there with the doctor, her prompt answer was:

"Why, we are married; did'nt you know it?"

She refused even to go to the table without my attendance, and when I was out visiting some patients, she waited for her meals till I came back. We stayed there but two days and returned together to Templeton.

A month afterward her brother was in Worcester, and stopped at this house. The landlord, after some conversation about general matters, said:

"So your sister is married to the Doctor?"

"I know nothing about it," was the reply.

This led to a full and altogether too free disclosure to the astonished brother about the particulars of our visit to the same house a month before, and his sister's representations that we were married. The brother immediately started for home, and repeated the story, as it was told to him, to his father and the family. Without seeing his daughter, the father at once procured a warrant, and had me arrested and brought before a justice on charge of seduction. The trial was brief; the daughter herself swore positively, that though she had been imprudent and indiscreet in going to Worcester with me, no improper communication had ever, there or elsewhere, taken place between us.

Of course, there was nothing to do but to let me go and I was discharged. But out of this affair came the worst that had yet fallen to my lot in life. The story got into the papers, with particulars and names of the parties, and in this way the people at Worthington, who had chased me as far as Hancock and had there lost all trace of me, found out where I was. If I had been aware of it, they might have looked elsewhere for me; but while I was felicitating myself upon my escape from the latest difficulty, down came an officer from Worthington with a warrant for my arrest. This officer, the sheriff, was connected with the family into which I had married in Worthington, and with him came two or three more relatives, all bound, as they boasted, to "put me through." They were excessively irate against me and very much angered, especially that their race after me to Hancock had been fruitless. I had fallen into the worst possible hands.

They took me to Northampton and brought me before a Justice, on a charge of bigamy: The sheriff who arrested me, and the relatives who accompanied him were willing to swear my life away, if they could, and the justice was ready enough to bind me over to take my trial in court, which was not to be in session for full six months to come. Those long, weary six months I passed in the county jail. Then came my trial. I had good counsel. There was not a particle of proof that I was guilty of bigamy; no attempt was made on the part of the prosecution to produce my first wife, from whom I had separated, or, indeed, to show that there was such a woman in existence. But, evidence or no evidence, with all Worthington against me, conviction was inevitable. The jury found me guilty. The judge promptly sentenced me to three years' imprisonment in the State Prison, at Charlestown, with hard labor, the first day to be passed in solitary confinement.

This severe sentence fairly stunned me. I was taken back to jail, and the following day I was conveyed to Charlestown with heavy irons on my ankles and handcuffed. No murderer would have been more heavily ironed. We started early in the morning, and by noon I was duly delivered to the warden at Charlestown prison. I was taken into the office, measured, asked my name, age, and other particulars, and then if I had a trade. To this I at once answered, "no." I wanted my twenty-four hours' solitary confinement in which to reflect upon the kind of "hard labor," prescribed in my sentence, I was willing to follow for the next three years; and I also wanted information about the branches of labor pursued in that prison. The next words of the warden assured me that he was a kind and compassionate man.

"Go," he said to an officer, "and instantly take off those irons when you take him inside the prison."

I was taken in and the irons were taken off. I was then undressed, my clothes were removed to another room, and I was redressed in the prison uniform. This was a grotesque uniform indeed. The suit was red and blue, half and half, like a harlequin's, and to crown all came a hat or cap, like a fool's cap, a foot and a half high and running up to a peak. Miserable as I was, I could scarcely help smiling at the utterly absurd appearance I knew I then presented. I even ventured to remark upon it; but was suddenly and sternly checked with the command:

"Silence! There's no talking allowed here."

Then began my twenty-four hours' solitary confinement, and twenty-four wretched hours they were. I had only bread and water to eat and drink, and I need not say that my unhappy thoughts would not permit me to sleep. At noon next day I was taken from my cell, and brought again before the warden, Mr. Robinson, who kindly said:

"You have no trade, you say; what do you want to go to work at?"

"Anything light; I am not used to hard labor," I replied.

So the warden directed that I should be put at work in the brush shop, where all kinds of brushes were made. Mr. Eddy was the officer in charge of this shop, and Mr. Knowles, the contractor for the labor employed in the brush business, was present. Both of these gentlemen took pains to instruct me in the work I was to begin upon, and were very kind in their manner towards me. I went to work in a bungling way and with a sad and heavy heart. At 12 o'clock we were marched from the shop to our cells, each man taking from a trap in the wall, as he went by, his pan containing his dinner, which consisted, that day, of boiled beef and potatoes. It was probably the worst dinner I had ever eaten, but I had yet to learn what prison fare was. From one o'clock to six I was in the shop again; then came Supper-mush and molasses that evening which was varied, as I learned afterwards, on different days by rye bread, or Indian bread and rye coffee. These things were also served for breakfast, and the dinners were varied on different days in the week. The fare was very coarse, always, but abundant and wholesome. After supper prisoners were expected to go to bed, as they were called out at six o'clock in the morning.

I stayed in the brush shop three or four months, but I made very little progress in learning the trade. I was willing enough to learn and did my best. From the day I entered the prison I made up my mind to behave as

L. A. Abbot

well as I could; to be docile and obedient, and to comply with every rule and order. Consequently I had no trouble, and the officers all treated me kindly. Warden Robinson was a model man for his position. He believed that prisoners could be reformed more easily by mild than by harsh measures - at least they would be more contented with their lot and would be subordinate. Every now and then he would ask prisoners if they were well treated by the officers; how they were getting on; if they had enough to eat, and so on. The officers seemed imbued with the warden's spirit; the chaplain of the prison, who conducted the Sunday, services and also held a Sunday school, was one of the finest men in the world, and took a personal interest in every prisoner. Altogether, it was a model institution. But in spite of good treatment I was intensely miserable; my mind was morbid; I was nearly, if not quite, insane; and one day during the dinner hour, I opened a vein in each arm in hopes that I should bleed to death. Bleed I did, till I fainted away, and as I did not come out when the other prisoners did, the officer came to my cell and discovered my condition. He at once sent for the Doctor who came and stopped the hemorrhage, and then sent me to the hospital where I remained two weeks.

After I came out of the hospitals the Warden talked to me about my situation and feelings. He advised me to go into the blacksmith shop, of course not dreaming that I knew anything of the work; but he said I would have more liberty there; that the men moved about freely and could talk to each other; that the work mainly was sharpening picks and tools, and that I could at least blow and strike. So I went into the blacksmith shop, and remained their six weeks. But, debilitated as I was, the work was too hard for me, and so the warden put me in the yard to do what I could. I also swept the halls and assisted in the cook-room. One day when the warden spoke to me, I told him that I knew something about taking care of the sick, and after some conversation, he transferred me to the hospital as a nurse.

Here, if there is such a things as contentment in prison, I was comparatively happy. I nursed the sick and administered medicines under direction of the doctor. I had too, with all easy position, more liberty than any other prisoner. I could go anywhere about the halls and yard, and in a few weeks I was frequently sent on an errand into the town. Everyone seemed to have the fullest confidence in me. The Warden talked to me whenever he saw me, and always had some kind word for me. One day I ventured to speak to him about his horse, of which he was very proud, and indeed the horse was a very fine one.

Mr. Warden, said I "that's a noble horse of yours; but he interferes badly, and that is only be- cause he is badly shod. If you will trust me, I can shoe him so as to prevent all that."

"Can you?" exclaimed the Warden in great surprise; "Well, if you can, I'll give you a good piece of bread and butter, or, anything else you want."

"I don't want your bread and butter," said I "but I will shoe your horse as he has never been shod before."

"Well take the horse to the shop and see what you can do."

Of course, I knew that by "bread and butter" the

L. A. Abbot

warden meant that if I could shoe his favorite horse so as to prevent him from interfering, he would gladly favor me as far as he could; and I knew, too, that I could make as good a shoe as any horse need wear. I gladly led the horse to the shop where I had so signally failed in pick and tool sharpening, and was received with jeers by my old comrades who wanted to know what I was going to do to that horse."

"O, simply shoe him," I said.

This greatly increased the mirth of my former shopmates; but their amusement speedily changed to amazement as they saw me make my nails, turn the shoes and neatly put them on. In due time the horse was shod, and I led him to the Warden for inspection; and before him and an officer who stood by him, I led the horse up and down to show that he did not interfere. The Warden's delight was unbounded; he never saw such a set of shoes; he declared that they fitted as if they had grown to the horse's hoofs. I need not say that from that day till the day I left the prison, I had everything I wanted from the Warden's own table; I fared as well as he did, and had favors innumerable.

About once a month I shod that horse, little thinking that he was to carry me over my three years' imprisonment in just half that time. Yet so it was. For talking now almost daily, in the hospital or in the yard, with the Warden, he became interested in me, and in answer to his inquiries I told him the whole story of my persecution, as I considered it, my trial and my unjust and severe sentence. When he had heard all he said:

"You ought not to be here another day; you ought

to go out."

The good chaplain also interested himself in my case, and after hearing the story, he and the Warden took a lawyer named Bemis, into their counsel, laid the whole matter before him and asked his opinion. Mr. Bemis, after hearing all the circumstances, expressed the belief that I might get a pardon. He entered into the matter with his whole heart. He sent for my son Henry and my first wife, and they came and corroborated my statement about the mutual agreement for separation, and told how long we had been parted. Mr. Bemis and they then went to Governor Briggs, and told him the story, and that I had served out half of my severe sentence, and pressed for a pardon. The Governor after due deliberation consented to their request. They came back to Charlestown with the joyful intelligence. Warden Robinson advised my son, that considering my present mental and physical condition, he had better break the intelligence gradually to me, and so Henry came to me and said, simply, that he thought he would soon have "good news" for me. The next day I was told that my pardon was certain. The day following, at 12 o'clock, I walked out, after eighteen months' imprisonment, a free man. I was in the streets of Charlestown with my own clothes on and five dollars, given to me by the Warden, in my pocket, I was poor, truly, but I was at liberty, and that for the day was enough.

CHAPTER III.

THE SCHEIMER SENSATION.

THE SCHEIMER FAMILY - IN LOVE WITH SARAH -
ATTEMPT TO ELOPE - HOW IT WAS PREVENTED - THE
SECOND ATTEMPT - A MIDNIGHT EXPEDITION - THE
ALARM - A FRIGHTFUL BEATING - ESCAPE - FLOGGING
THE DEVIL OUT OF SARAH - WINTER IN NEW
HAMPSHIRE - RETURN TO NEW JERSEY - "BOSTON
YANKEE" - PLANS TO SECURE SARAH.

I went at once to the Prisoners Home, where I was
kindly received, and I stayed there two days. The
superintendent then paid my passage to Pittsfield
where I wished to go and meet my son. From Pittsfield
I went to Albany, then New York, and from there to
Newtown N. J. Here I went into practice, meeting with
almost immediate success, and staid there two months.
It was my habit to go from town to town to attend to
cases of a certain class and to sell my vegetable
preparations; and from Newtown I went to Belvidere,
stopping at intermediate towns on the way, and from
Belvidere I went to Harmony, a short distance below,
to attend a case of white swelling, which I cured.

Now just across the Delaware - river, nine miles above
Easton. Penn., lived a wealthy Dutch farmer, named
Scheimer, who heard Of the cure I had effected in
Harmony, and as he had a son, sixteen years of age,

afflicted in the same way, he sent for me to come and see him. I crossed the river, saw the boy, and at Scheimer's request took up my residence with him to attend to the case. He was to give me, with my board, five hundred dollars if I cured the boy; but though the boy recovered under my treatment, I never received my fee for reasons which will appear anon. I secured some other practice in the neighborhood, and frequently visited Easton, Belvidere, Harmony, Oxford, and other near by places, on either side of the river.

The Scheimer family consisted of the "old folks" and four sons and four daughters, the children grown up, for my patient, sixteen years old, was the youngest. The youngest daughter, Sarah, eighteen years old, was an accomplished and beautiful girl. Now it would seem as if with my sad experience I ought by this time, to have turned my back on women forever. But I think I was a monomaniac on the subject of matrimony. My first wife had so misused me that it was always in my mind that some reparation was due me, and that I was fairly entitled to a good helpmate. The ill-success of my efforts, hitherto, to secure one, and my consequent sufferings were all lost upon me - experience, bitter experience, had taught me nothing.

I had not been in the Scheimer family three months before I fell in love with the daughter Sarah and she returned my passion. She promised to marry me, but said there was no use in saying anything to her parents about it; they would never consent on account of the disparity in our ages, for I was then forty years old; but she would marry me nevertheless, if we had to run away together. Meanwhile, the old folks had seen enough of our intimacy to suspect that it might lead to something yet closer, and one day Mr. Scheimer invited me to leave his house and not to return. I asked for one last interview with Sarah, which was accorded, and we then arranged a plan by which she should meet me the next afternoon at four o'clock at the Jersey ferry, a mile below the house, when we proposed to quietly cross over to Belvidere and get married. I then took leave of her and the family and went away.

The next day, at the appointed time, I was at the ferry - Sarah, as I learned afterwards, left the house at a much earlier hour to "take a walk" and while she was, foolishly I think, making a circuitous route to reach the ferry, her father, who suspected that she intended to run away, went to the ferryman and told him his suspicions, directing him if Sarah came there by no means to permit her to cross the river. Consequently when Sarah met me at the ferry, the ferryman flatly refused to let either of us go over. He knew all about it, he said, and it was "no go." I had two hundred dollars in my pocket and I offered him any reasonable sum, if he would only let us cross; but no, he knew the Scheimers better than he knew me, and their goodwill was worth more than mine. Here was a block to the game, indeed. I had sent my baggage forward in the morning to Belvidere; Sarah had nothing but the clothes she wore, for she was so carefully watched that she could carry or send nothing away; but she was ready to go if the obstinate ferryman had not prevented us.

While we were pressing the ferryman to favor us, down came one of Sarah's brothers with a dozen neighbors, and told her she must return home or he would carry her back by force. I interfered and said she should not go. Whereupon one fellow took hold of me and I promptly knocked him down, and notified the crowd hat the first who laid hands on me, or who attempted to take her home violently, would get a dose from my pistol which I then exhibited:

"Sarah must go willingly or not at all," said I.

The production of my pistol, the only weapon in the crowd, brought about a new state of affairs, and the brother and others tried persuasion; but Sarah stoutly insisted that she would not return. "Now hold on," boys, said I, "I am going to say something to her." I then took her aside and told her that there was no use in trying to run away then; that she had better go home quietly, and tell the folks that she was sorry for what she bad done, that she had broken off with me, and would have nothing more to do with me; that I would surely see her to-morrow, and then we could make a new plan. So she announced her willingness to go quietly home with her brother and she did so. I went to a public house half a mile below the ferry. That night the gang came down to this house with the intention of driving me away from the place, or, possibly, of doing something worse; but while they were howling outside, the landlord sent me to my room and then went out and told the crowd I had gone away.

The next morning I boldly walked up to Scheimer's house to get a few books and other things I had left there, and I saw Sarah. I told her to be ready on the following Thursday night and I would have a ladder against her window for her to escape by. She promised to be ready. Meantime, though I had been in the house but a few minutes, some one who had seen me go in gathered the crowd of the day before, and the first thing I knew the house was beseiged. Mrs. Scheimer had gone up stairs for my things. I went out and faced

L. A. Abbot

the little mob. I was told to leave the place or they would kill me. One of Sarah's brothers ran into the house, brought out a musket and aimed it at me; but it missed fire. I drew my pistol the crowd keeping well away then, and told him that if he did not instantly bring that musket to me I would shoot him. He brought it, and I threw it over the fence, Sarah crying out from the window, "good! good!" The mob then turned and abused and blackguarded her. Then the old lady came out, bringing a carpet bag containing my books and things, asking me to see if "it was all right." I had no disposition to stop and examine just then; I told the mob I had no other business there; that I was going away, and to my surprise, I confess, I was permitted to leave the place unmolested.

It is quite certain the ferryman made no objection to my crossing, and I went to Belvidere where I remained quietly till the appointed Thursday night, when I started with a trusty man for Scheimer's. We timed our journey so as to arrive there at one o'clock in the morning. Ever since her attempt to elope, Sarah had been watched night and day, and to prevent her abduction by me, Mr. Scheimer had two or three men in the house to stand guard at night. Sarah was locked in her room, which is precisely what we had provided for, for no one in the house supposed that she could escape by the window. There was a big dog on the premises, but he and I were old friends, and he seemed very glad to see me when I came on the ground on this eventful night. Sarah was watching, and when I made the signal she opened the window and threw out her ready prepared bundle. Then my man and I set the ladder and she came safely to the ground. A moment more and we would have stolen away, when, as ill luck would have it, the ladder fell with a great crash, and the infernal dog, that a moment before seemed almost in our confidence, set up a howl and then barked loud enough to wake the dead.

Forthwith issued from the house old Scheimer, two of his sons and his hired guard-a half dozen in all. There was a time then. The girl was instantly seized and taken into the house. Then all hands fell upon us two, and though I and my man fought our best they managed to pound us nearly to death. The dog, too, in revenge no doubt for the scare the ladder had given him, or perhaps to show his loyalty to his master, assisted in routing us, and put in a bite where he could. It is a wonder we were not killed. Sarah, meanwhile, was calling out from the house, and imploring them not to murder us. How we ever got away I hardly know now, but presently we found ourselves in the road running for our lives, and running also for the carriage we had concealed in the woods, half a mile above. We reached it, and hastily unhitching and getting in we drove rapidly for the bridge crossing over to Belvidere. That beautiful August night had very few charms for us. It would have been different indeed if I had succeeded in securing my Sarah; and to think of having the prize in my very grasp, and the losing all!

We reached the hotel in Belvidere at about half-past two o'clock in the morning, wearied, worn, bruised and disheartened. My man had not suffered nearly as severely as I had; the bulk of their blows fell upon me, and I had the sorest body and the worst looking face I had ever exhibited. I rested one day and then hurried on to New York. Of course, I had no means of knowing the feelings or condition of the loved girl from whom I had been so suddenly and so violently parted. I only learned from an Easton man whom I knew and whom I met in the city, that "Sarah Scheimer was sick"-that was all; the man said he did'nt know the family very well, but he had heard that Miss Scheimer had been "out of her head, if not downright crazy."

Crazy indeed! How mad and how miserable that poor girl was made by her own family, I did not know till months afterward, and then I had the terrible story from her own lips. It seems that when her father and his gang returned from pursuing me, as they did a little way up the road towards Belvidere, they found her almost frantic. They locked her up in her room that night with no one to say so much as a kind word to her. How she passed that night, after the scenes she had witnessed, and the abuse with which her father and brothers had loaded her before they thrust her into her prison, may be imagined. The next day she was wrought up to a frenzy. Her parents pronounced her insane, and called in a Dutch doctor who examined her and said she was "bewitched!" And this is the remedy he proposed as a cure; he advised that she should be soundly flogged, and the devil whipped out of her. Her family, intensely angered at her for the trouble she had made them, or rather had caused them to make for themselves, were only too glad to accept the advice. The old man and two sons carried a sore bruise or two apiece they got from me the night before, and seized the opportunity to pay them off upon her. So they stripped her bare, and flogged her till her back was a mass of welts and cuts, and then put her to bed. That bed she never left for two months, and then came out the shadow of her former self. But the Dutch doctor declared that the devil was whipped out of her, and that she was entirely cured. A few months afterward the family had the best of reasons for believing that they had whipped the devil into her, instead of out of her.

After staying in New York a few days, I went to Dover, N.H., where I had some acquaintances, and where I hoped to get into a medical practice, which, with the help of my friends, I did very soon. I lived quietly in that place all winter, earning a good living and laying by some money. During the whole time I never heard a word from Sarah. I wrote at least fifty letters to her, but as I learned afterward, and, indeed, surmised at the time, every one of them was intercepted by her father or brothers, and she did not know where I was and so could not write to me. I left Dover in May and went down to New York. I had some business there which was soon transacted, and early in June I went over to New Jersey-to Oxford, a small place near Belvidere.

This place I meant to make my base of operations for the new campaign I had been planning all winter. I "put up" at a public house kept by a man who was known in the region round about as the "Boston Yankee," for he migrated from Boston to New Jersey and was doing a thriving business at hotel keeping in Oxford. What a thorough good-fellow he was will presently appear. I had been in the hotel four days and had become pretty intimate with the landlord before I ventured to make inquiries about what I was most anxious to learn; but finally I asked him if he knew the Scheimers over the river? He looked at me in a very comical way, and then broke out:

"Well, I declare, I thought I knew you, you're the chap that tried to run away with old Scheimer's daughter Sarah, last August; and you're down here to get her this time, if you can."

I owned up to my identity, but warned Boston Yankee

that if he told any one who I was, or that I was about there, I'd blow his brains out.

"You keep cool," said he, "don't you be uneasy; I'm your friend and the gal's friend, and I'll help you both all I can; and if you want to carry off Sarah Scheimer and marry her, I'll tell you how to work it. You see she has been watched as closely as possible all winter, ever since she got well, for she was crazy-like, awhile. Well, you could'nt get nearer to her, first off, than you could to the North Pole; but do you remember Mary Smith who was servant gal, there when you boarded with Scheimer?" I remembered the girl well and told him so, and he continued: "Well, I saw her the other day, and she told me she was living in Easton, and where she could be found; now, I'll give you full directions and do you take my horse and buggy to-morrow morning early and go down and see her, and get her to go over and let Sarah know that you're round; meantime I'll keep dark; I know my business and you know yours."

I need not say how overjoyed I was to find this new and most unexpected friend, and how gratefully I accepted his offer. He gave me the street, house and number where Mary Smith lived and during the evening we planned together exactly how the whole affair was to be managed, from beginning to end. I went to bed, but could scarcely sleep; and all night long I was agitated by alternate hopes and fears for the success of the scheme of to-morrow.

CHAPTER IV.

SUCCESS WITH SARAH.

MARY SMITH AS A CONFEDERATE - THE PLOT - WAITING IN THE WOODS - THE SPY OUTWITTED - SARAH SECURED - THE PURSUERS BAFFLED - NIGHT ON THE ROAD - EFFORTS TO GET MARRIED - THE "OLD OFFENDER" MARRIED AT LAST - A CONSTABLE AFTER SARAH - HE GIVES IT UP - AN ALE ORGIE - RETURN TO "BOSTON YANKEE'S" - A HOME IN GOSHEN.

It was Saturday morning, and after an early breakfast I was on the road with Boston Yankee's fast horse; towards Easton. On my arrival there I had no difficulty in finding Mary Smith, who recognized me at once, and was very glad to see me. She knew I had come there to learn something about Sarah; she had seen her only a week ago; she was well again, and the girls had talked together about me. This was pleasant to hear, and I at once proposed to Mary to go to Scheimer's and tell Sarah that I was there; I would give her ten dollars if she would go. "O! she would gladly serve us both for nothing."

So she made herself ready, got into the buggy, and we started for Scheimer's. When we were well on the road I said to her:

"Now, Mary, attend carefully to what I say: you will

need to be very cautious in breaking the news to Sarah that I am here; she has already suffered a great deal on my account, and may be very timid about my being in the neighborhood; but if she still loves me as you say she does, she will run any risk to see me, and, if I know her, she will be glad to go away with me. Now, this is what you must do; you must see her alone and tell her my plan; here, take this diamond ring; she knows it well; manage to let her see it on your finger; then tell her that if she is willing to leave home and marry me, I will be in the woods half a mile above her house to-morrow afternoon at 5 o'clock, with a horse and buggy ready to carry her to Belvidere. If she will not, or dare not come, give her the ring, and tell her we part, good friends, forever."

It was a beautiful afternoon as we drove along the road. We talked about Sarah and old times, and I made her repeat my instructions over and over again and she promised to convey every word to Sarah. We neared Scheimer's house about six o'clock, and when we were a little way from there I told Mary to get out, so as to excite no suspicions as to who I was; she did so, and I waited till I saw her go into the house, and then drove rapidly by towards the Belvidere bridge, and was safely at Oxford by nightfall. I told my friend, the landlord, what I had done, and he said that everything was well planned. He also promised to go with me next day to assist me if necessary, and, said he:

"If everything is all right, do you carry off the girl and I'll walk up to Belvidere; but don't bring Sarah this way-head toward Water Gap. When you're married fast and sure, you can come back here as leisurely as you're a mind to, and nobody can lay a hand upon you or her."

We arranged some other minor details of our expedition and I went to bed.

The next afternoon at four o'clock I was at the appointed place, and Boston Yankee was with me. I did not look for Sarah before five o'clock, so we tied our horse and kept a good watch upon the road. An hour went by and no Sarah appeared. I told Boston Yankee I did not believe she would come.

"Don't be impatient; wait a little longer," said my friend.

In twenty minutes we saw emerge, not from Scheimer's house, but from his eldest son's house, which was still nearer to the place where we were waiting, three women, two of whom I recognized as Sarah and Mary, and the third I did not know, nor could I imagine why she was with the other two; but as I saw them, leaving Boston Yankee in the woods, I drove the horse down into the road. As Sarah drew near she kissed her hand to me and came up to the wagon. "Are you ready to go with me?" I asked. "I am, indeed," was her reply, and I put out my hand to help her into the buggy. But the third woman caught hold of her dress, tried to prevent her from getting in, and began to scream so as to attract attention at Sarah's brother's house. I told the woman to let her go, and threatened her with my whip. "Get away," shouted Boston Yankee, who had come upon the scene. "Drive as fast as you can; never mind if you kill the horse."

We started; the woman still shouting for help, and I drove on as rapidly as the horse would go. When we had gone on a mile or two, I asked Sarah what all this meant? She told me that the woman was her brother's servant; that Mary and herself left her father's house a little after four o'clock to go over and call at her brother's; that just before five, when she was to meet me, she and Mary proposed to go out for a walk; that the whole family watched her constantly, and so her brother's wife told the servant woman to get on her things and go with them. "You, may be sure," she, added, "that the woman will arouse the whole neighborhood, and that they will all be after us." I needed no further hint to push on. We were going toward Water Gap, as Boston Yankee had advised, and when we were about eight miles on the way, I deemed it prudent to drive into the woods and to wait till night before going on. We drove in just off the road, and tied our horse. We were effectually concealed; our pursuers, if there were any, would be sure to go by us, and meantime we could talk over our plans for the future. Sarah told me that when Mary came to the house the night before, she was not at all surprised to see her, as she occasionally came up from Easton to make them a little visit, and to stay all night; that she went to the summer-house with Mary to sit down and talk, and almost immediately saw the ring on Mary's finger; that when she saw it she at once recognized it, and asked her: "O! Mary, where did you get that ring?" "Keep quiet," said Mary: "don't talk loud, or some one may hear you; don't be agitated; your lover is near, and has sent me to tell you." It was joyful news to Sarah, and how readily she had acquiesced in my plan for an elopement was manifest in the fact that she was then by my side.

We bad not been in the woods an hour when, as I anticipated, we heard our pursuers, we did not know how many there were, drive rapidly by. "Now we can go on, I suppose," said Sarah. "Oh no, my dear," I replied, "now is just the time to wait quietly here;" and wait we did till 'eight o'clock, when our pursuers, having gone on a few miles, and having seen or learned nothing of the fugitives, came by again "on the back track." They must have thought we had turned off into some other road. I waited a while longer to let our friend's get a little nearer home and further away from us, and then took the road again toward Water Gap.

We reached Water Gap at midnight, had some supper and fed the horse. We rested awhile, and then drove leisurely on nine miles further, where we waited till daylight and crossed the river. We were in no great hurry now; we were comparatively safe from pursuit. We soon came to a public, house, where we stopped and put out the horse, intending to take breakfast. While I was inquiring of the landlord if there was a justice of the peace in the neighborhood, the landlord's wife had elicited from Sarah the fact of our elopement, who she was, who her folks were, and so on. The well-meaning landlady advised Sarah to go back home and get her parents consent before she married. Sarah suggested that the very impossibility of getting such consent was the reason for her running away; nor did it appear how she was to go back home alone even if she desired to. We saw that we could get no help there, so I countermanded my order for breakfast, offering at the same time to pay for it as if we had eaten it, ordered out my horse and drove on. After riding some ten miles we arrived at another public house on the road, and as the landlord come out to the door I immediately asked him where I could find a justice of the peace? He laughed, for he at once comprehended the whole situation, and said:

"Well, well! I am an old offender myself; I ran away

with my wife; there is a justice of the peace two miles from here, and if you'll come in I'll have him here within an hour."

We had reached the right place at last, for while the landlady was getting breakfast for us, and doing her best to make us comfortable and happy, the Old Offender himself took his horse and carriage and went for the justice. By the time we had finished our breakfast he was back with him, and Sarah and I were married in "less than no time," the Old Offender and his wife singing the certificate as witnesses. I never paid a fee more gladly. We were married now, and all the Scheimers in Pennsylvania were welcome to come and see us if they pleased.

No Scheimers came that day; but the day following came a deputation from that family, some half dozen delegates, and with them a constable from Easton, with a warrant to arrest Sarah for something-I never knew what-but at any rate he was to take her home if necessary by force. The Old Offender declined to let these people into his house; Sarah told me to keep out of the way and she would see what was wanted. Whereupon she boldly went to the door and greeted those of her acquaintances who were in the party. The constable knew her, and told her he had come to take her home. "But what if I refuse to go?" "Well then, I have a warrant to take you; but if you are married, I have no power over you." Well married I am, said Sarah, and she produced the certificate, and the Old Offender and his wife came out and declared that they witnessed the ceremony.

What was to be done? evidently nothing; only the constable ordered a whole barrel of ale to treat his posse and any one about tire town who chose to drink, and the barrel was rolled out on the grass, tapped, and for a half hour there was a great jollification, which was not exactly in honor of our wedding, but which afforded the greatest gratification to the constable, his retainers, and those who happened to gather to see what was going on. This ended, and the bill paid, the Easton delegation got into their wagons and turned their horses heads towards home.

We passed three delightful days under the Old Offender's roof, and then thanking our host for his kindness to us, and paying our bill, we started on our return journey for Oxford. We arrived safely, and staid with Boston Yankee a fortnight. We were close by the Scheimer homestead, which was but a few miles away across the river; but we feared neither father nor brothers, nor even the woman who was so unwilling to let Sarah go with me. The constable, and the rest had carried home the news of our marriage, and the old folks made the best of it. Indeed, after they heard we had returned to Oxford, Sarah's mother sent a man over to tell her that if she would come home any day she could pack her clothes and other things, and take them, away with her. The day after we received this invitation, Boston Yankee offered to take Sarah over home, and promised to bring her safely back. So she went, was treated tolerably well, at any rate, she secured her clothes and brought them home with her.

It was now time to bid forewell to our staunch friend, Boston Yankee. I had inducements to go to Goshen, Orange County, N. Y., where I had many acquaintances, and to Goshen we went. We found a good boarding place, and I began to practice medicine, After we had been there a while, Sarah wrote home to let her

L. A. Abbot

family know where she was, and that she was well and happy. Her father wrote in reply that we both might come there at any time, and that if she would come home he would do as well by her as he would by any of his children. This letter made Sarah uneasy. In spite of all the ill usage she had received from her parents and family, she was nevertheless homesick, and longed to get back again. I could see that this feeling grew upon her daily. We were pleasantly situated where we were; I had a good and growing practice, and we had made many friends; but this did not satisfy her; she had some property in her own right, but her father was trustee of it, and he had hitherto kept it away from her from spite at her love affair with me. But now she was to be taken into favor again, and she represented to me that we could go back and get her money, and that I could establish myself there as well as anywhere; we could live well and happily among her friends and old associations. These things were dinged in my ears day after day, till I was sick of the very sound. I could see that she was bound, or, as the Dutch doctor would have said, "bewitched" to go back, and at last, after five happy months in Goshen, in an evil hour I consented to go home with her.

CHAPTER V.

HOW THE SCHEIMERS MADE ME SUFFER.

RETURN TO SCHEIMER - PEACE AND THEN PANDEMONIUM - FRIGHTFUL FAMILY ROW - RUNNING FOR REFUGE - THE GANG AGAIN - ARREST AT MIDNIGHT - STRUGGLE WITH MY CAPTORS - IN JAIL ONCE MORE - PUT IN IRONS - A HORRIBLE PRISON BREAKING OUT - THE DUNGEON - SARAH'S BABY - CURIOUS COMPROMISES - OLD SCHEIMER MY JAILER - SIGNING A BOND - FREE AGAIN - LAST WORDS FROM SARAH.

We went back to the Scheimer homestead and were favorably received. There was no special enthusiasm over our return, no marked demonstrations of delight; but they seemed glad to see us, and all the unpleasant things of the past, if not forgotten, were tacitly ignored on all sides. We passed a pleasant evening together in what seemed a re-united family circle-one of the brothers only was absent-and next morning we met cordially around the breakfast table. I really began to think it was possible that all the old difficulties might be healed, and that the pleasant picture Sarah painted, at Goshen, about settling down happily in Pennsylvania, could be fully realized.

After breakfast I took a conveyance to go three or four miles to see a man who owed me some money for medical services in his family, and was away from Scheimer's three or four hours. During this brief absence I could not help thinking with genuine satisfaction of the happiness Sarah was experiencing in the gratification of her longing to return home again. Surely, I thought, she must be happy now. No more homesickness, and a full and complete reconciliation with her family; all the anger, abuse, and blows forgotten or forgiven; she restored to her place in the family; and even her objectionable husband received with open arms.

But what an enormous difference there is between fancy and fact. During this brief absence of mine, had come home the brother who had always seemed to concentrate the hatred of the whole family towards me for the wrong they assumed I had done to the youngest daughter who loved me. On my return I found the peaceful home I left in the morning a perfect pandemonium. Sarah was fairly frantic. The whole family were abusing her. The returned brother especially, was calling her all the vile names he could lay his tongue to. I learned afterwards that he had been doing it ever since he came into the house that day and found her at home and heard that I was with her. They had picked, wrenched rather, out of her the secret I had confided to her that I had another wife from whom I was "separated," but not divorced. My sudden presence on this scene was not exactly oil on troubled waters; it was gunpowder to fire. As soon as Sarah saw me at the door she cried out:

"O! husband, let us go away from here."

Her mother turned and shouted at me that I had better fly at once or they would kill me. Meanwhile, that mob, which the Scheimer boys seemed always to have at hand, was gathering in the dooryard. I managed to get near enough to Sarah to tell her that I would send a man for her next day, and then if she was willing to come with me she must get away from her family if possible. I then made a rush through the crowd, and reached the road. I think the gang had an indistinct knowledge of the situation, or they would have mobbed me, and perhaps killed me. They knew something was "to pay" at Scheimer's, but did not know exactly what. Once on the road it was my intention to have gone over to Belvidere, and then on to Oxford, where I should have found a sure refuge with my friend Boston Yankee.

Would that I had done so; but I was a fool; I thought I could be of service to Sarah by remaining near her; might see her next day; I might even be able to get her out of the house, and then we could once more elope together and go back again to Goshen where we had been so happy. So I went to a public house three miles above Scheimer's, and remained there quietly during the rest of the day, revolving plans for the deliverance of Sarah. I thought only of her. It is strange that I did not once realize what a perilous position I was in myself- that, firmly as I believed myself to be wedded to Sarah, I was in fact amenable to the law, and liable to arrest and punishment. All this never occurred to me. I saw one or two of the gang who were at Scheimer's about the hotel, but they did not offer to molest me, and I paid no particular attention to them. I did not know then that they were spies and were watching my movements. At nine o'clock I went to bed. At midnight, or thereabouts, I was roughly awakened and told to get up. Without waiting for me, to comply, five men who had entered my room pulled me out of bed, and almost before I could huddle on my clothes I was handcuffed. Then one of them, who said he was a constable from Easton, showed a warrant for my arrest. What the arrest was for I was not informed. I was taken down stairs, put into a wagon, the men followed, and the horses started in the direction of Easton. By Scheimer's on the way, and I could see a light in Sarah's window. I remembered how in, all the Bedlam in the house that morning she still cried out: "I will go with him." I remembered how, only a few months before, she had been brutally flogged in that very chamber, to "get the devil out of her." I remembered, too, the many happy, happy hours we had passed together. And here was I, handcuffed and dragged in a wagon, I knew not whither.

This for thoughts-in the way of action, was all the while trying to get my handcuffs off, and at last I succeeded in getting one hand free. Waiting my opportunity till we came to a piece of woods, I suddenly jumped up and sprang from the wagon. It was a very dark night, and in running into the woods I struck against a tree with such force as to knock me down and nearly stun me. Two of the men were on me in an instant. After a brief struggle I managed to get away and ran again. I should have escaped, only a high rail fence brought me to a sudden stop, and I was too exhausted to climb over it. My pursuers who were hard at my heels the whole while now laid hold of me. In the subsequent struggle I got out my pocket knife, and stabbed one of them, cutting his arm badly. Then they overpowered me. They dragged me to the roadside, brought a rope out of the wagon, bound my arms and legs, and so at last carried me to Easton.

It was nearly daylight when I was thrust into jail. There

were no cells, only large rooms for a dozen or more men, and I was put, into one of these with several prisoners who were awaiting trial, or who had been tried and were there till they could be sent to prison. It was a day or two before I found out what I was there for. Then a Dutch Deputy Sheriff, who was also keeper of the jail, came and told me that I was held for bigamy, adding the consoling intelligence that it would be a very hard job for me, and that I would get five or six years in State prison sure. I was well acquainted in Easton, and I sent for lawyer Litgreave for assistance and advice. I sent also to my half-sister in Delaware County, N. Y., and in a day or two she came and saw me, and gave Mr. Litgreave one hundred dollars retaining fee. My lawyer went to see the Scheimers and when he returned he told me that he hoped to save me from State prison-at all events he would exercise the influence he had over the family to that end; but I must expect to remain in jail a long time. Precisely what this meant I did not know then; but I found out afterwards.

Soon after this visit from the lawyer, the Deputy Sheriff came in and said that he was ordered "by the Judge" to iron me, and it was done. They were heavy leg-irons weighing full twelve pounds, and I may say here that I wore them during the whole term of my imprisonment in this jail, or rather they wore me - wearing their way in time almost into the bone. I had been here a week now, and was well acquainted with the character of the place. It was indescribably filthy; no pretence was made of cleansing it. The prisoners were half fed, and, at that, the food was oftentimes so vile that starving men rejected it. The deputy who kept the jail was cruel and malignant, and took delight in torturing his prisoners. He would come in sometimes under pretence of looking at my irons to see if they were safe, and would twist and turn them about so that I suffered intolerable pain, and blood flowed from my wounds made by these cruel irons. Such abuse as he could give with his tongue he dispensed freely. Of course he was a coward, and he never dared to come into one of the prisoner's rooms unless he was armed. This is a faithful photograph of the interior of the jail at Easton, Penn., as it was a few years ago; there may have been some improvement since that time; for the sake of humanity, I hope there has been.

After I had been in this jail about six weeks, and had become well acquainted with my room-mates, I communicated to them one day, the result of my observation:

"There," said I, showing them a certain place in the wall," is a loose stone that with a little labor can be lifted out, and it will leave a hole large enough for us to get out of and go where we like."

Examination elicited a unanimous verdict in favor of making the attempt. With no tools but a case knife we dug out the mortar on all sides of the stone doing the work by turns and covering the stone by hanging up an old blanket-which excited no sus picion, as it was at the head of one of the iron bedsteads - whenever the Deputy or any of his men were likely to visit us. In twelve days we completed the work, and could lift out the stone. The hole was large enough to let a man through, and there was nothing for us to do but to crawl out one after the other and drop down a few feet into the yard. This yard was surrounded by a board fence that could be easily surmounted. I intended to take the lead, after taking off my irons (which I had learned to do, and indeed, did every day, putting them on only when I was liable to be "inspected") and after leaving these irons at the Deputy's door, I intended to put myself on the Jersey side of the river as speedily as possible.

Liberty was within reach of every man in that room, and the night was set for the escape. But one of the crowd turned traitor, and, under pretence, of speaking to the Deputy about some matter, managed to be called out of the room and disclosed the whole. The man was waiting transportation to prison to serve out a sentence of ten years, and, with the chance of escape before him, it seemed singular that he should reveal a plan which promised to give him liberty; but probably he feared a failure; or that he might be recaptured and his prison sentence increased; while on the other hand by disclosing the plot he could curry favor enough to get his term reduced, and perhaps he might gain a pardon. Any how, he betrayed us. The Deputy came in and found the stone in the condition described, and forthwith we were all removed to the dungeon, or dark room, and kept there on bread and water for twelve days. We heard afterwards that our betrayer did get five years less than his original sentence for subjecting his comrades in misery to twelve days of almost indescribable suffering. We were not only in a totally dark and frightfully filthy hole, but we were half starved, and the Deputy daily took delight in taunting us with our sufferings.

At the end of the twelve days we were taken back to the old room where we found the stone securely fastened in with irons. Moreover, we were now under stricter observation, and at stated hours every day, an inspector came in and examined the walls. This soon wore off, however, and when the inspection was finally abandoned, about two months from the time of our first attempt, we managed to find another place in the old wall where we could dig out and we went to work. We were a fortnight at it, and had nearly completed our labor when we were discovered.

This time we spent fourteen days in the dungeon for our pains.

And now comes an extraordinary disclosure with regard to my imprisonment. A few days after my removal from the dungeon to the old quarters again, the Deputy, in one of his rare periods of what, with him, passed for good humor, informed me that Sarah had been confined, and had given birth to a fine boy; that she was crying for my release; that Lawyer Sitgreave was interceding for me; but that the old man Scheimer was still obstinate and would not let me out. Passing over my feelings with regard to the birth of my son, here was a revelation indeed! It will be remembered that I had only been told that I was under indictment for bigamy. I had never been brought before, a justice for a preliminary examination; never bound over for trial; and now it transpired that old Scheimer, a Pennsylvania Dutch farmer, had the power to put me in jail, put me in irons, and subject me to long months, perhaps years of imprisonment. I had something to occupy my thoughts now, and for the remaining period of my jail life.

Next came a new dodge of the Scheimers, the object of which was to show that Sarah's marriage to me was no marriage at all, thus leaving her free to marry any other man her family might force upon her. When I had been in jail seven months, one day the Deputy came in and said that he was going to take off my irons. I told him I wouldn't trouble him to do that, for though I had worn them when he and his subordinates were around till the irons had nearly killed me, yet at other times I had been in a habit of taking them off at pleasure; and to prove it, I sat down and in a few minutes handed him the irons. The man was amazed; but saying nothing about the irons, he approached me on another subject. He said he thought if I would sign an acknowledgment that I was a married man when I married Sarah Scheimer, and would leave the State forever, I could get out of jail; would I do it? I told him I would give no answer till I had seen my counsel.

Well, the next day Lawyer Sitgreave came to me and told me I had better do it, and I consented. Shortly afterwards, I was taken to court, for the first time in this whole affair, and was informed by the judge that if I would sign a bond not to go near the Scheimer house or family he would discharge me. I signed such a bond, and the judge then told me I was discharged; but that I ought to have gone to State prison for ten years for destroying the peace and happiness of the Scheimer family. Truly the Scheimer family were a power, indeed, in that part of the country!

My lawyer gave me five dollars and I went to Harmony and staid that night. The next day I went to an old friend of mine, a Methodist minister, and persuaded him to go over and see what Sarah Scheimer's feelings were towards me, and if she was willing to come to me with our child. He went over there, but the old Scheimers suspected his errand, and watched him closely to see that he held no communication with Sarah. He did, however, have an opportunity to speak to her, and she sent me word that if she could ever get her money and get away from her parents, she would certainly join me in any part of the world. I was warned, at the same time, not to come near the house, for fear that her father or some of her brothers would kill me.

CHAPTER VI.

FREE LIFE AND FISHING.

TAKING CARE OF CRAZY MEN - CARRYING OFF A BOY - ARRESTED FOR STEALING MY OWN HORSE AND BUGGY - FISHING IN LAKE WINNIPISEOGEE - AN ODD LANDLORD - A WOMAN AS BIG AS A HOGSHEAD - REDUCING THE HOGSHEAD TO A BARREL - WONDER-FUL VERIFICATION OF A DREAM - SUCCESSFUL MEDICAL PRACTICE - A BUSY WINTER IN NEW HAMPSHIRE - BLANDISHMENTS OF CAPTAIN BROWN - I GO TO NEWARK, NEW JERSEY.

The next day I left Harmony and walked to Port Jarvis, on the Erie Railroad, N. Y., arriving late at night, and entirely footsore, sick, and disheartened. I went to the hotel, and the next morning I found myself seriously sick. Asking advice, I was directed to the house of a widow, who promised to nurse and take care of me. I was ill for two weeks, and meantime, my half- sister in Delaware County, to whom I made known my condition, sent me money for my expenses, and when I had sufficiently recovered to travel, I went to this sister's house in Sidney, and there I remained several days, till I was quite well and strong again.

Casting about for something to do, a friend told me that he knew of an opportunity for a good man at Newbury to take care of a young man, eighteen years of age, who was insane. I went there and saw his father, and he put him under my charge. I had the care of him four months, and during the last two months of the time I traveled about with him, and returned him, finally, to his friends in a materially improved condition. The friends of another insane man in Montgomery, near Newbury, hearing of my success with this young man, sent for me to come and see them. I went there and found a man who had been insane seven years, but who was quiet and well-behaved, only he was "out of his head." I engaged to do what I could for him. The father of my Newbury patient had paid me well, and with my medical practice and the sale of medicines in traveling about, I had accumulated several hundred dollars, and when I went to Montgomery I had a good horse and buggy which cost me five hundred dollars. So, when my new patient had been under my care and control two months, I proposed that he should travel about with me in my buggy, and visit various parts of the State in the immediate vicinity. His friends thought well of the suggestion, and we traveled in this way about four months, stopping a few days here and there, when I practiced where I could, and sold medicines, making some money. At the end of this time I went back to Montgomery with my patient, as I think, fully restored, and his father, besides, paying the actual expenses of our journey, gave me six hundred dollars.

Returning to Sidney I learned that my first and worst wife was then living with the children at Unadilla, a few miles across the river in Otsego County. I had no desire to see her, but I heard at the same time that my youngest boy, a lad ten years old, had been sent to work on a farm three miles beyond, and that he was not well taken care of. I drove over to see about it, and after some inquiry I was told that the boy was then in school. Going to the schoolhouse and asking for him, the school-mistress, who knew me, denied that he was there, but I pushed in, and found him, and a ragged, miserable looking little wretch he was. I brought him out, put him into the carriage and took him with me on the journey which I was then contemplating to Amsterdam, N. Y., stopping at the first town to get him decently clothed. The boy went with me willingly, indeed he was glad to go, and in due time we arrived at Amsterdam, and from there we went to Troy.

I had not been in Troy two hours before I was arrested for stealing my own horse and buggy! My turnout was taken from me, and I found myself in durance vile. I was not long in procuring bail, and I then set myself, to work to find out what this meant. I was shown a handbill describing my person, giving my name, giving a description of my horse, and offering a reward of fifty dollars for my arrest. This was signed by a certain Benson, of Kingston, Sullivan County, N.Y. I then remembered that while I was traveling with my insane patient from Montgomery through Sullivan County, I fell in with a Benson who was a very plausible fellow, and who scraped acquaintance with me, and while I was at Kingston he rode about with me on one or two occasions. One day he told me that he knew a girl just out of the place who was subject to fits, and wanted to know if I could do anything for her; that her father was rich and would pay a good price to have her cured. I went to see the girl and did at least enough to earn a fee of one hundred dollars, which her father gladly paid me. Benson also introduced me to some other people whom I found profitable patients. I thought he was a very good friend to me, but he was a cool, calculating rascal. He meant to rob me of my horse and buggy, and went deliberately to work about it. First, he issued the handbill which caused my arrest in Troy, where he knew I was going. Next, as appeared when he came up to Troy to prosecute the suit against me, he forged a bill of sale. The case was tried and decided in my favor. Benson appealed, and again it was decided that the horse belonged to me. I then had him indicted for perjury and forgery, and he was put under bonds of fourteen hundred dollars in each case to appear for trial. Some how or other he never appeared, and whether he forfeited his bonds, or otherwise slipped through the "meshes of the law," I never learned, nor have I ever seen him since he attempted to swindle me. But these proceedings kept me in Troy more than a month, and to pay my lawyer and other expenses, I actually sold the horse and buggy the scoundrel tried to steal from me.

Taking my boy to Sidney and putting him under the care of my half sister, I went to Boston, where I met two friends of mine who were about going to Meredith Bridge, N.H., to fish through the ice on Lake Winnipiseogee. It was early in January, 1853, and good, clear, cold weather. They represented the sport to be capital, and said that plenty of superb lake trout and pickerel could be taken every day, and urged me to go with them. As I had nothing special to do for a few days, I went. When we reached Meredith we stopped at a tavern near the lake, kept by one of the oddest landlords I have ever met. After a good supper, as we were sitting in the barroom, the landlord came up to me and at once opened conversation in the following manner:

"Waal, where do you come from, anyhow?"

"From Boston," I replied.

"Waal, what be you, anyhow?"

"Well, I practice medicine, and take care of the sick."

"Dew ye? Waal, do ye ever cure anybody?"

"O, sometimes; quite frequently, in fact."

"Dew ye! waal, there's a woman up here to Lake Village,'Squire Blaisdell's wife, who has had the dropsy more'n twelve years; been filling' all the time till they tell me she's bigger'n a hogshead now, and she's had a hundred doctors, and the more doctors she has the bigger she gets; what d' ye think of that now?"

I answered that I thought it was quite likely, and then turned away from the landlord to talk to my friends about our proposed sport for to-morrow, mentally making note of 'Squire Blaisdell's wife in Lake Village.

After breakfast next morning we went out on the lake, cut holes in the ice, set our lines, and before dinner we had taken several fine trout and pickerel, the largest and finest of which we put into a box with ice, and sent as a present to President Pierce, in Washington. We had agreed, the night before, to fish for him the first day, and to send him the best specimens we could from his native state. After dinner my friends started to go out on the ice again, and I told them "I guess'd I wouldn't go with them, I had fished enough for that day." They insisted I should go, but I told them I preferred to take a walk and explore the country. So they went to the lake and I walked up to Lake Village.

L. A. Abbot

I soon found Mr. Blaisdell's house, and as the servant who came to the door informed me that Mr. Blaisdell was not at home, I asked to see Mrs. Blaisdell, And was shown in to that lady. She was not quite the "hogshead" the landlord declared her to be, but she was one of the worst cases of dropsy I had ever seen. I introduced myself to her, told her my profession, and that I had called upon her in the hope of being able to afford her some relief; that I wanted nothing for my services unless I could really benefit her.

"O, Doctor," said she, "you can do nothing for me; in the past twelve years I have had at least forty different doctors, and none of them have helped me."

"But there can be no harm in trying the forty-first;" and as I said it I took from my vest pocket and held out in the palm of my hand some pills:

"Here, madame, are some pills made from a simple blossom, which cannot possibly harm you, and which, I am sure, will do you a great deal of good."

"O, Mary!" she exclaimed to her niece, who was in attendance upon her, "this is my dream! I dreamed last night that my father appeared to me and told me that a stranger would come with a blossom in his hand; that he would offer it to me, and that if I would take it I should recover. Go and get a glass of water and I will take these pills at once."

"Surely," said Mary, "you are not going to take this stranger's medicine without knowing anything about it, or him?"

"I am indeed; go and get the water."

She took the medicine and then told me that her father, who had died two years ago, was a physician, and had carefully attended to her case as long as he lived; but that she had a will of her own, and had sent far and near for other doctors, though with no good result.

"You have come to me," she continued, "and although I am not superstitious, your coming with a blossom in your hand, figuratively speaking, is so exactly in accordance with my dream, that I am going to put myself under your care."

She then asked me if I lived in the neighborhood, and I told her no; that I had merely come up from Boston with two friends to try a few days' fishing through the ice on the lake.

"You can fish to better purpose here, I think," she said; "you can get plenty of practice in the villages and farm houses about here: at any rate, stay for the present and undertake my case, and I will pay you liberally."

I went back to Meredith Bridge-I believe it is now called Laconia-and had another day's fishing with my friends. When they were ready to pack up and return to Boston, I astonished them by informing them that I should stay where I was for the present, perhaps for months, and that I believed I could find a good practice in Meredith and adjoining places. So they left me and I went to Lake Village, and made that pleasant place my headquarters.

The weeks wore on, and if Mrs. Blaisdell was a hogshead, as the Meredith landlord said, when I first saw her, she soon became a barrel under my treatment, and in four months she was entirely cured, and was as sound as any woman in the State. I had as much other business too as I could attend to, and was very busy and happy all the time.

In May I went to Exeter, alternating between there and Portsmouth, and finding enough to do till the end of July. While I was in Portsmouth on one of my last visits to that place, I received a call from a sea-captain by the name of Brown, who told me that he had heard of my success in dropsical cases, and that I must go to Newark, N. J., and see his daughter. "Pay," he said, "was no object; I must go." I told him that I had early finished my business in that vicinity, and that when I went to New York, as I proposed to do shortly, I would go over to Newark and see his daughter. A few days afterward, when I had settled my business and collected my bills in Portsmouth and Exeter, I went to New York, and from there to Newark.

CHAPTER VII.

WEDDING A WIDOW,
AND THE CONSEQUENCES.

I MARRY A WIDOW - SIX WEEKS OF HAPPINESS - CONFIDING A SECRET AND THE CONSEQUENCES - THE WIDOW'S BROTHER - SUDDEN FLIGHT FROM NEWARK - IN HARTFORD, CONN. - MY WIFE'S SISTER BETRAYS ME - TRIAL FOR BIGAMY - SENTENCED TO TEN YEARS IMPRISONMENT - I BECOME A "BOBBIN BOY" - A GOOD FRIEND - GOVERNOR PRICE VISITS ME IN PRISON - HE PARDONS ME - TEN YEARS' SENTENCE FULFILLED IN SEVEN MONTHS.

Why in the world did Captain Brown ever tempt me with the prospect of a profitable patient in Newark? I had no thought of going to that city, and no business there except to see if I could cure Captain Brown's daughter. With my matrimonial monomania it was like putting my hand into the fire to go to a fresh place, where I should see fresh faces, and where fresh temptations would beset me. And when I went to Newark, I went only as I supposed, to see a single patient; but Captain Brown prevailed upon me to stay to take care of his daughter, and assured me that he and his friends would secure me a good practice. They did. In two months I was doing as well in my profession as I had ever done in any place where I had located. I might have attended strictly to my business, and in a few years have acquired a handsome competence. But, as ill luck, which, strangely enough, I then considered good luck, would have it, when I had been in Newark some two months, I became acquainted with a buxom, good-looking widow, Mrs. Elizabeth Roberts. I protest to-day that she courted me-not I her. She was fair, fascinating, and had a goodly share of property. I fell into the snare. She said she was lonely; she sighed; she smiled, and I was lost.

Would that I had observed the elder Weller's injunction: "Bevare of vidders;" would that I had never seen the Widow Roberts, or rather that she had never seen me. Eight weeks after we first met we were married. We had a great wedding in her own house, and all her friends were present. I was in good practice with as many patients as I could attend to; she had a good home and we settled down to be very happy.

For six weeks, only six weeks, I think we were so. We might have been so for six weeks, six months, six years longer; but alas! I was a fool I confided to her the secret of my first marriage, and separation, and she confided the same secret to her brother, a well-to-do wagon-maker in Newark. So far as Elizabeth was concerned, she said she didn't care; so long as the separation was mutual and final, since so many years had elapsed, and especially since I hadn't seen the woman for full six years, and was not supposed to know whether she was alive or dead, why, it was as good as a divorce; so reasoned Elizabeth, and it was precisely my own reasoning, and the reasoning which had got me into numberless difficulties, to say nothing of jails and prisons. But the brother had his doubts about it, and came and talked to me on the subject several times. We quarrelled about it. He threatened to have me arrested for bigamy. I told him that if he took a step in that direction I would flog him. Then he had me brought before a justice for threatening him, with a view to having me put under bonds to keep the peace. I employed a lawyer who managed my case so well that the justice concluded there was no cause of action against me.

But this lawyer informed me that the brother was putting, even then, another rod in pickle for me, and that I had better clear out. I took his advice, I went to the widow's house, packed my trunk, gathered together what money I could readily lay hands upon, and with about $300 in my pocket, I started for New York, staying that night at a hotel in Courtland street.

The following morning I went over to Jersey City, hired a saddle-horse, and rode to Newark. The precise object of my journey I do not think I knew myself; but I must have had some vague idea of persuading Elizabeth to leave Newark and join me in New York or elsewhere. I confess, too, that I was more or less under the influence of liquor, and considerably more than less. However, no one would have noticed this in my appearance or demeanor. I rode directly to Elizabeth's door, hitched my horse, and went into the house. The moment my wife saw me she cried out:

"For God's sake get out of this house and out of town as soon as you can; they have been watching for you ever since yesterday; they've got a warrant for your arrest; don't stay here one moment."

I asked her if she was willing to follow me, and she said she would do so if she only dared but her brother had made an awful row, and had sworn he would put me in prison anyhow; I had better go back to New York and await events. I started for the door, and was unhitching my horse, when the brother and a half dozen more were upon me. I sprang to the saddle. They tried to stop me; the over-eager brother even caught me by the foot; but I dashed through the crowd and rode like mad to Jersey City, returned the horse to the livery stable, crossed the ferry to New York, went to my hotel, got my trunk, and started for Hartford, Conn., where I arrived in the evening.

This was in the month of June, 1854. I went to the old Exchange Hotel in State street, and very soon acquired a good practice. Indeed, it seems as if I was always successful enough in my medical business-my mishaps have been in the matrimonial line. When I had been in Hartford about three months, and was well settled, I thought I would go down to New York and see a married sister of Elizabeth's, who was living there, and try to find out how matters were going on over in Newark. That I found out fully, if not exactly to my satisfaction, will appear anon.

When I called at the sister's house, the servant told me she was out, but would be back in an hour; so I left my name, promising to call again. I returned again at one o'clock in the afternoon, and the sister was in, but declined to see me. As I was coming down the steps, a policeman who seemed to be lounging on the opposite side of the street, beckoned to me, and suspecting nothing, I crossed over to see what he wanted. He simply wanted to know my name, and when I gave it to him he informed me that I was his prisoner. I asked for what? and he said "as a fugitive from justice in New Jersey."

This was for taking the pains to come down from Hartford to inquire after the welfare of my wife! whose sister, the moment the servant told her I had been there, and would call again, had gone to the nearest police station and given information, or made statements, which led to the setting of this latest trap for me. The policeman took me before a justice who sent me to the Tombs. On my arrival there I managed to pick up a lawyer, or rather one of the sharks of the place picked me up, and said that for twenty-five dollars he would get me clear in three or four hours. I gave him the money, and from that day till now, I have never set eyes upon him. I lay in a cell all night, and next morning Elizabeth's brother, to whom the sister in New York had sent word that I was caged, came over from Newark to see me. He said he felt sorry for me, but that he was "bound to put me through." He then asked me if I would go over to Newark without a requisition from the Governor of New Jersey, and I told him I would not; whereupon he went away without saying another word, and I waited all day to hear from the lawyer to whom I had given twenty-five dollars, but he did not come.

So next day when the brother came over and asked me the same question, I said I would go; wherein I was a fool; for I ought to have reflected that he had had twenty-four hours in which to get a requisition, and that he might in fact have made application for one already, without getting it, and every delay favored my chances of getting out. But I had no one to advise me, and so I went quietly with him and an officer to the ferry, where we crossed and went by cars to Newark. I was at once taken before a justice, who, after a hearing of the case, bound me over, under bonds of only one thousand dollars, to take my trial for bigamy.

If I could have gone into the street I could have procured this comparatively trifling bail in half an hour; as it was, after I was in jail I sent for a man whom I knew, and gave him my gold watch and one hundred dollars, all the money I had, to procure me bail, which he promised to do; but he never did a thing for me, except to rob me.

A lawyer came to me and offered to take my case in hand for one hundred dollars, but I had not the money to give him. I then sent to New York for a lawyer whom I knew, and when he came to see me he took the same view of the case that Elizabeth and I did; that is, that the long separation between my first wife and myself, and my presumed ignorance as to whether she was alive or dead, gave me full liberty to marry again. At least, he thought any court would consider it an extenuating circumstance, and he promised to be present at my trial and aid me all he could.

I lay in Newark jail nine months, awaiting my trial. During that time I had almost daily quarrels with the jailor, who abused me shamefully, and told me I ought to go to State prison and stay there for life. Once he took hold of me and I struck him, for which I was put in the dark cell forty-eight hours. At last came my trial. The court appointed counsel for me, for I had no money to fee a lawyer, and my New York friend was on hand to advise and assist. I lad witnesses to show the length of time that had elapsed since my separation from my first wife, and we also raised the point as to whether the justice who married me, was really a legal justice of the peace or not. The trial occupied two days. I suppose all prisoners think so, but the Judge charged against me in every point; the jury was out two hours, and then came in for advice on a doubtful question; the judge gave them another blast against me, and an hour after they came in with a verdict of "guilty." I went back to jail and two days afterwards was brought up for sentence which was - "ten years at hard labor in the State prison at Trenton."

Good heavens! All this for being courted and won by a widow!

The day following, I was taken in irons to Trenton. The Warden of the prison, who wanted to console me, said that, for the offence, my sentence was an awful one, and that he didn't believe I would be obliged to serve out half of it. As I felt then, I did not believe I should live out one-third of it. After I had gone through the routine of questions, and had been put in the prison uniform, a cap was drawn down over my face, as if I was about to be hung, and I was led, thus blind-folded, around and around, evidently to confuse me, with regard to the interior of the prison-in case I might ever have any idea of breaking out. At last I was brought to a cell door and the cap was taken off. There were, properly no "cells" in this prison-at least I never saw any; but good sized rooms for two prisoners, not only to live in but to work in. I found myself in a room with a man who was weaving carpets, and I was at once instructed in the art of winding yarn on bobbins for him-in fact, I was to be his "bobbin- boy."

I pursued this monotonous occupation for two months, when I told the keeper I did not like that business, and wanted to try something that had a little more variety in it. Whereupon he put me at the cane chair bottoming business, which gave me another room and another chum, and I remained at this work while I was in the prison. In three weeks I could bottom one chair, while my mate was bottoming nine or ten as his day's work; but I told the keeper I did not mean to work hard, or work at all, if I could help it. He was a very nice fellow and he only laughed and let me do as I pleased. Indeed, I could not complain of my treatment in any re- spect; I had a good clean room, good bed, and the fare was wholesome and abundant. But then, there was that terrible, terrible sentence of ten long years of this kind of life, if I should live through it.

After I had been in prison nearly seven months, one day a merchant tailor whom I well knew in Newark, and who made my clothes, including my wedding suit when I married the Widow Roberts, came to see me. The legislature was in session and he was a member of the Senate. He knew all the circumstances of my case, and was present at my trial. After the first salutation, he laughingly said:

"Well, Doctor, those are not quite as nice clothes as I used to furnish you with."

"No," I replied, "but perhaps they are more durable."

After some other chaff and chat, he made me tell him all about my first marriage and subsequent separation, and after talking awhile he went away, promising to see me soon. I looked upon this only as a friendly visit, for which I was grateful; and attached no great impor- tance to it. But he came again in a few days, and after some general conversation, he told me that there was a movement on foot in my favor, which might bring the best of news to me; that he had not only talked with his friends in the legislature, and enlisted their sympathy and assistance, but he had laid the whole circum- stances, from beginning to end, before Governor Price;

that the Governor would visit the prison shortly, and then I must do my best in pleading my own cause.

In a day or two the Governor came, and I had an opportunity to relate my story. I told him all about my first unfortunate marriage, and the separation. He said that he knew the facts, and also that he had lately received a letter from my oldest son on the subject, and had read it with great interest. I then appealed to the Governor for his clemency; my sentence was an outrageously severe one, and seemed almost prompted by private malice; I implored him to pardon me; I went down on my knees before him, and asked his mercy. He told me to be encouraged; that he would, be in the prison again in a few days, and he would see me. He then went away.

I at once drew up a petition which my friend in the Senate circulated in the legislature for signatures, and afterwards sent it to Newark, securing some of the best names in that city. It was then returned to me, and two weeks afterwards when the Governor came again to the prison I presented it to him, and he put it in his pocket.

In two days' time, Governor Price sent my pardon into the prison. The Warden came and told me of it, and said he would let me out in an hour. Then came a keeper who once more put the cap over my face and led me around the interior-I was willingly led now-till he brought me to a room where he gave me my own clothes which I put on, and with a kind parting word, and five dollars from the Warden, I was soon in the street, once more a free man. My sentence of ten years had been fulfilled by an imprisonment of exactly seven months.

L. A. Abbot

I went and called on Governor Price to thank him for his great goodness towards me. He received me kindly, talked to me for some time, and gave me some good advice and a little money. With this and the five dollars I received from the Warden of the prison I started for New York.

CHAPTER VII.

ON THE KEEN SCENT.

GOOD RESOLUTIONS - ENJOYING FREEDOM - GOING AFTER A CRAZY MAN - THE OLD TEMPTER IN A NEW FORM - MARY GORDON - MY NEW "COUSIN" - ENGAGED AGAIN - VISIT TO THE OLD FOLKS AT HOME - ANOTHER MARRIAGE - STARTING FOR OHIO - CHANGE OF PLANS - DOMESTIC QUARRELS - UNPLEASANT STORIES ABOUT MARY - BOUND OVER TO KEEP THE PEACE - ANOTHER ARREST FOR BIGAMY - A SUDDEN FLIGHT - SECRETED THREE WEEKS IN A FARM HOUSE - RECAPTURED AT CONCORD - ESCAPED ONCE MORE - TRAVELING ON THE UNDERGROUND RAILROAD - IN CANADA.

It would seem as if, by this time, I had had enough of miscellaneous marrying and the imprisonment that almost invariably followed. I had told Governor Price, when I first implored him for pardon, that if he would release me I would begin a new life, and endeavor to be in all respects a better man. I honestly meant to make every effort to be so, and on my stay to New York I made numberless vows for my own future good behavior. I bound myself over, as it were, to keep the pace - my own peace and quiet especially - and became my own surety. That I could not have had a poorer bondsman, subsequent events proved to my sorrow. But I started fairly, and meant to let liquor alone; to attend strictly to my medical business, which I always managed to make profitable, and above all, to have nothing to do with women in the love-making or matrimonial way.

With those good resolutions I arrived in New York and went to my old hotel in Courtland Street, where I was well known and was well received. My trunk, which I had left there sixteen months before, was safe, and I had a good suit of clothes on my back - the clothes I took off when I went to prison in Trenton -and which were returned to me when I came away. I went to a friend who loaned me some money, and I remained two or three days in town to try my new-found freedom, going about the city, visiting places of amusement, enjoying myself very much, and keeping, so far, the good resolutions I had formed.

From New York I went to Troy, and at the hotel where I stopped I became acquainted with a woman who told me that her husband was in the Insane Asylum at Brattleboro, Vt. She was going to see him, and if he was fit to be removed, she proposed to take him home, with her. I told her of the success I had had in taking care of two men at Newbury and Montgomery; and how I had traveled about the country with them, and with the most beneficial results to my patients. She was much interested, inquired into the particulars, and finally thought the plan would be a favorable one for her husband. She asked me to go with her to see him, and said that if he was in condition to travel he should go about with me if he would; at any rate, if he came out of the Asylum she would put him under my care. We went together to Brattleboro, and the very day we arrived her husband was taken in an apoplectic fit from which he did not recover. She carried home his corpse, and I lost my expected patient.

But I must have something to do for my daily support, and so I went to work and very soon sold some medicines and recipes, and secured a few patients. I also visited the adjoining villages, and in a few weeks I had a very good practice. I might have lived here quietly and made money. Nobody knew anything of my former history, my marriages or my misfortunes, and I was doing well, with a daily increasing business. And so I went on for nearly three months, gaining new acquaintances, and extending my practice every day.

Then came the old tempter in a new form, and my matrimonial monomania, which I hoped was cured forever, broke out afresh. One day, at the public house where I lived, I saw a fine girl from New Hampshire, with whom I became acquainted - so easily, so far as she was concerned - that I ought to have been warned to have nothing to do with her; but, as usual, in such cases, my common sense left me, and I was infatuated enough to fancy that I was in love.

Mary Gordon was the daughter of a farmer living near Keene, N. H., and was a handsome girl about twenty years of age. She was going, she told me, to visit some friends in Bennington, and would be there about a month, during which time, if I was in that vicinity, she hoped I would come and see her. We parted very lovingly, and when she had been in Bennington a few days she wrote to me, setting a time for me to visit her; but in business in Brattleboro was too good to leave, and I so wrote to her. Whereupon, in another week, she came back to Brattleboro and proposed to finish the remainder of her visit there, thus blinding her friends at home who would think she was all the while at Bennington.

Our brief acquaintance when she was at the house before, attracted no particular attention, and when she came now I told the landlord that she was my cousin, and he gave her a room and I paid her bills. The cousin business was a full cover to our intimacy; she sat next to me at the table, rode about with me to see my patients, and when I went to places near by to sell medicine, and we were almost constantly together. Of course, we were engaged to be married, and that very soon.

In a fortnight after her arrival I went home with her to her father's farm near Keene, and she told her mother that we were "engaged." The old folks thought they would like to know me a little better, but she said we were old friends, she knew me thoroughly, and meant to marry me. There was no further objection on the part of her parents, and in the few days following she and her mother were busily engaged in preparing her clothes and outfit.

I then announced my intention of returning to Brattleboro to settle up my business in that place, and she declared she would go with me; I was sure to be lonesome; she might help me about my bills, and so on. Strange as it may seem, her parents made no objection to her going, though I was to be absent a fortnight, and was not to be married till I came back. So we went together, and I and my "cousin" put up at the hotel we had lately left. For two weeks I was busy in making my final visits to my patients acquaintances, she generally going with me every day.

At the end of that time we went back to Keene, and in three weeks we were married in her father's house, the old folks making a great wedding for us, which was attended by all the neighbors and friends of the family. We stayed at home two weeks, and meanwhile arranged our plans for the future. We proposed to go out to Ohio, where she had some relatives, and settle down. She had seven hundred dollars in bank in Keene which she drew, and we started on our journey. We went to Troy, where we stayed a few days, and during that time we both concluded that we would not go West, but return to Keene and live in the town instead of on the farm, so that I could open an office and practice there.

So we went back to her home again, but before I completed my plans for settling down in Keene, Mary and I had several quarrels which were worse than mere ordinary matrimonial squabbles. Two or three young men in Keene, with whom I had become acquainted, twitted me with marrying Mary, and told me enough about her to convince me that her former life had not been altogether what it should have been. I had been too blinded by her beauty when I first saw her in Brattleboro, to notice how extremely easily she was won. Her parents, too, were wonderfully willing, if not eager, to marry her to me. All these things came to me now, and we had some very lively conversations on the subject, in which the old folks joined, siding with their daughter of course. By and by the girl went to Keene and made a complaint that she was afraid of her life, and I was brought before a magistrate and put under bonds of four hundred dollars to keep the peace. I gave a man fifty dollars to go bail for me, and then, instead of going out to the farm with Mary, I went to the hotel in Keene.

The well-known character of the girl, my marriage to her, the brief honeymoon, the quarrels and the cause of the same, were all too tempting material not to be served up in a paragraph, and as I expected and feared, out came the whole story in the Keene paper.

This was copied in other journals, and presently came letters to the family and to other persons in the place, giving some account of my former adventures and marriages. Of this however I knew nothing, till one day, while I was at the hotel, I was suddenly arrested for bigamy. But I was used to this kind of arrest by this time, and I went before the magistrate with my mind made up that I must suffer again for my matrimonial monomania.

It was just after dinner when I was arrested, and the examination, which was a long one, continued till evening. Every one in the magistrate's office was tired out with it, I especially, and so I took a favorable opportunity to leave the premises. I bolted for the door, ran down stairs into the street, and was well out of town before the astonished magistrate, stunned constable, and amazed spectators realized that I had gone.

Whether they than set out in pursuit of me I never knew, I only know they did not catch me. I ran till I came to the house of a farmer whom I had been attending for some ailment, and hurriedly narrating the situation, I offered one hundred dollars if he would secrete me till the hue and cry was over and I could safely get away. I think he would have done it from good will, but the hundred dollar bill I offered him made the matter sure. He put my money into his pocket, and be put me into a dark closet, not more than five feet square, and locked me in.

I stayed in that man's house, never going out of doors, for more than three weeks, and did my best to board out my hundred dollars. The day after my flight the whole neighborhood was searched, that is, the woods, roads, and adjacent villages. They never thought of looking in a house, particularly in a house so near the town; and, as I heard from my protector, they telegraphed and advertised far and near for me.

I anticipated all this, and for this very reason I remained quietly where I was, in an unsuspected house, and with my dark closet to retire to whenever any one came in; and gossiping neighbors coming in almost every hour, kept me in that hole nearly half the time. I heard my own story told in that house at least fifty times, and in fifty different ways.

At last, when I thought it was safe, one night my host harnessed up his horses and carried me some miles on my way to Concord. He drove as far as he dared, for he wanted to get back home by daylight, so that his expedition might excite no suspicion. Twenty miles away from Keene he set me down in the road, and, bidding him "good-bye," I began my march toward Concord. When I arrived there, almost the first man I saw in the street was a doctor from Keene. I did not think he saw me, but he did, as I soon found out, for while I was waiting at the depot to take the cars to the north, I was arrested.

The Keene doctor owed me a grudge for interfering, as he deemed it; with his regular practice, and the moment he saw me he put an officer on my trail. I thought it was safe here to take the cars, for I was footsore and weary, nor did I get away from Keene as fast and as far as I wanted to. I should have succeeded but for that doctor.

When the officer brought me before a justice, the doctor was a willing witness to declare that I was a fugitive from justice, and he stated the circumstances of my escape. So I was sent back to Keene under charge of the very officer who arrested me at the depot.

I would not give this officer's name if I could remember it, but he was a fine fellow, and was exceedingly impressible. For instance, on our arrival at Keene, he allowed me to go to the hotel and pack my trunk to be forwarded to Meredith Bridge by express. He then handed me over to the authorities, and I was immediately taken before the magistrate from whom I had previously escaped, the Concord officer accompanying the Keene officer who had charge of me.

The examination was short; I was bound over in the sum of one thousand dollars to take my trial for bigamy. On my way to jail I persuaded the Concord officer-with a hundred dollar bill which I slipped into his hand-to induce the other officer to go with me to the hotel under pretense of looking after my things, and getting what would be necessary for my comfort in jail. My Concord friend kept the other officer down stairs-in the bar-room, I presume - while I went to my room. I put a single shirt in my pocket; the distance from my window to the ground was not more than twelve or fifteen feet, and I let myself down from the window sill and then dropped.

I was out of the yard, into the street, and out of town in less than no time. It was already evening, and everything favored my escape. I had no idea of spending months in jail at Keene, and months more, perhaps years, in the New Hampshire State Prison. All my past bitter experiences of wretched prison life urged me to flight.

And fly I did. No stopping at the friendly farmer's, my former refuge, this time; that would be too great a risk. No showing of myself in any town or villege where the telegraph might have conveyed a description of my person. I traveled night and day on foot, and more at night than during the day, taking by-roads, lying by in the woods, sleeping in barns, and getting my meals in out-of-the-way farm houses.

I had plenty of money; but this kind of travelling is inexpensive, and, paying twenty-five cents for one or two meals a day, as I dared to get them, and sleeping in barns or under haystacks for nothing, my purse did not materially diminish. I was a good walker, and in the course of a week from the night when I left Keene, I found myself in Biddeford, Maine.

There was some sense of security in being in another State, and here I ventured to take the cars for Portland, where I staid two days, sending in the meantime for my trunk from Meredith Bridge, and getting it by express. Of course it went to a fictitious address at Meredith, and it came to me under the same name which I had registered in my hotel at Portland.

I did not mean to stay there long. My departure was hastened by the advice of a man who knew me, and told he also knew my New Hampshire scrape, and that I had better leave Portland as soon as possible. Half an hour after this good advice I was on my way by cars to Canada. In Canada I stayed in different small towns near the border, and "kept moving," till I thought the

New Hampshire matter had blown over a little, or at least till they had given me up as a "gone case," and I then reappeared in Troy.

CHAPTER IX.

MARRYING TWO MILLINERS.

BACK IN VERMONT - FRESH TEMPTATIONS - MARGARET BRADLEY - WINE AND WOMEN - A MOCK MARRIAGE IN TROY - THE FALSE CERTIFICATE - MEDICINE AND MILLINERY - ELIZA GURNSEY - A SPREE AT SARATOGA - MARRYING ANOTHER MILLINER - AGAIN ARRESTED OR BIGAMY - IN JAIL ELEVEN MONTHS - A TEDIOUS TRIAL - FOUND GUILTY - APPEAL TO SUPREME COURT - TRYING TO BREAK OUT OF JAIL - A GOVERNOR'S PROMISE - SECOND TRIAL - SENTENCE TO THREE YEARS' IMPRISONMENT.

From Troy I went, first to Newburyport, Mass., where I had some business, and where I remained a week, and then returned to Troy again. Next I went to Bennington, Vt., to sell medicines and practice, and I found enough to occupy me there for full two months. From Bennington to Rutland, selling medicines on the way, and at Rutland I intended to stay for some time. My oldest son was there well established in the medical business, and I thought that both of us together might extend a wide practice and make a great deal of money.

No doubt we might have done so, if I had minded my medical business only, and had let matrimonial matters alone. I had just got rid of a worthless woman in New Hampshire with a very narrow escape from State prison. But, as my readers know by this time, all experience, even the bitterest, was utterly thrown away upon me; I seemed to get out of one scrape only to walk, with my eyes open, straight into another.

At the hotel where I went to board, there was temporarily staying a woman, about thirty-two years old, Margaret Bradly, by name, who kept a large millinery establishment in town. I became acquainted with her, and she told me that she owned a house in the place, in which she and her mother lived; but her mother had gone away on a visit, and as she did not like to live alone she had come to the hotel to stay for a few days till her mother returned. Margaret was a fascinating woman; she knew it, and it was my miserable fate to become intimate, altogether too intimate with this designing milliner.

I went to her store every day, sometimes two or three times a day, and she always had in her backroom, wine or something stronger to treat me with, and in the evening I saw her at the hotel. When her mother came back, and Margaret opened her house again, I was a constant visitor. I was once more caught; I was in love.

Matters went on in this way for several weeks, when one evening I told her that I was going next day to Troy on business, and she said she wanted to go there to buy some goods, and that she would gladly take the opportunity to go with me, if I would let her. Of course, I was only too happy; and the next day I and my son, and she and one of the young women in her employ, who was to assist her in selecting goods, started for Troy. When I called for her, just as we were leaving the house, the old lady, her mother, called out:

"Margaret, don't you get married before you come back."

"I guess I will," was Margaret's answer, and we went, a very jovial party of four, to Troy and put up at the Girard House, where we had dinner together, and drank a good deal of wine. After dinner my son and myself went to attend to our business, she and her young woman going to make their purchases, and arranging to meet us at a restaurant at half past four o'clock, when we would lunch preparatory to returning to Rutland.

We met at the appointed place and hour, and had a very lively lunch indeed, an orgie in fact, with not only enough to eat, but altogether too much to drink. I honestly think the two women could have laid me and my son under the table, and would have done it, if we had not looked out for ourselves; as it was, we all drank a great deal and were very merry. We were in a room by ourselves, and when we had been there nearly an hour, it occurred to Margaret that it would be a good idea to humor the old lady's dry joke about the danger of our getting married during this visit to Troy.

"Henry "said she to my son; "Go out and ask the woman who keeps the saloon where you can get a blank marriage certificate, and then get one and bring it here, and we'll have some fun."

We were all just drunk enough to see that there was a joke in it, and we urged the boy to go. He went to the woman, who directed him to a stationer's opposite, and presently he came in with a blank marriage certificate. We called for pen and ink and he sat down and filled out the blank form putting in my name and Margaret

Bradley's, signing it with some odd name I have forgotten as that of the clergyman performing the ceremony. He then signed his own name as a witness to the marriage, and the young woman who was with us also witnessed it with her signature. We had a great deal of fun over it, then more wine, and then it was time for us to hurry to the depot to take the six o'clock train for Rutland.

Reaching home at about eleven o'clock at night, we found the old lady up, and waiting for Margaret. We went in and Margaret's first words were:

"Well, mother! I'm married; I told you, you know, I thought I should be; and here's my certificate."

The mother expressed no surprise-she knew her daughter better than I did, then-but quietly congratulated her, while I said not a single word. My son went to see his companion home, and, as I had not achieved this latest greatness, but had it thrust upon me, I and my new found "wife" went to our room. The next day I removed from the hotel to Margaret's house and remained there during my residence in Rutland, she introducing me to her friends as her husband, and seeming to consider it an established fact.

Three weeks after this mock marriage, however, I told Margaret that I was going to travel about the State a while to sell my medicines, and that I might be absent for some time. She made no objections, and as I was going with my own team she asked me to take some mantillas and a few other goods which were a little out of fashion, and see if I could not sell them for her. To be sure I would, and we parted on the best of terms.

Behold rue now, not only a medical man and a marrying man, but also a man milliner. When I could not dispose of my medicines, I tried mantillas, and in the course of my tour I sold the whole of Margaret's wares, faithfully remitting to her the money for the same. I think she would have put her whole stock of goods on me to work off in the same way; but I never gave her the opportunity to do so.

My journeying brought me at last to Montpelier where I proposed to stay awhile and see if I could establish a practice. I had disposed of my millinery goods and had nothing to attend to but my medicines - alas that my professional acquirements as a marrying man should again have been called in requisition. But it was to be. It was my fate to fall into the hands of another milliner.

"Insatiate monster! would not one suffice?"

It seems not. There was a milliner at Rutland whose family and, friends all believed to be my wife, though she knew she was not; and here in Montpelier, was ready waiting, like a spider for a fly, another milliner who was about to enmesh me in the matrimonial net. I had not been in the place a week before I became acquainted with Eliza Gurnsey. I could hardly help it, for she lived in the hotel where I stopped, and although she was full thirty-five years old, she was altogether the most attractive woman in the house. She was agreeable, good-looking, intelligent, and what the vernacular calls "smart." At all events, she was much too smart for me, as I soon found out.

She had a considerable millinery establishment which she and her younger sister carried on, employing several women, and she was reputed to be well off.

Strange as it may seem in the light of after events, she actually belonged to the church and was a regular attendant at the services. But no woman in town was more talked about, and precisely what sort of a woman she was may be estimated from the fact that I had known her but little more than a week, when she proposed that she, her sister and I should go to Saratoga together, and have a good time for a day or two.

I was fairly fascinated with the woman and I consented. The younger sister was taken with us, I thought at first as a cover, I knew afterwards as a confederate, and Eliza paid all the bills, which were by no means small ones, of the entire trip. We stopped in Saratoga at a hotel, which is now in very different hands, but which was then kept by proprietors who, in addition to a most excellent table and accommodations, afforded their guests the opportunity, if they desired it, of attending prayers every night and morning in one of the parlors. This may have been the inducement which made Eliza insist upon going to this house, but I doubt it.

For our stay at Saratoga, three or four days, was one wild revel. We rode about, got drunk, went to the Lake, came back to the hotel, and the second day we were there, Eliza sent her sister for a Presbyterian minister, whose address she had somehow secured, and this minister came to the hotel and married us. I presume I consented, I don't know, for I was too much under the effect of liquor to know much of anything. I have an indistinct recollection of some sort of a ceremony, and after- wards Eliza showed me a certificate-no Troy affair, but a genuine document signed by a minister residing in Saratoga, and witnessed by her sister and some one in the hotel who had been called in. But the whole was like a dream to me; it was the plot of an infamous woman to endeavor to make herself respectable by means of a marriage, no matter to whom or how that marriage was effected.

Meanwhile, the Montpelier papers had the whole story, one of them publishing a glowing account of my elopement with Miss Gurnsey, and the facts of our marriage at Saratoga was duly chronicled. This paper fell into the hands of Miss Bradley, at Rutland, and as she claimed to be my wife, and had parted with me only a little while before, when I went out to peddle medicines and millinery, her feelings can be imagined. She read the story and then aroused all Rutland. I had not been back from Saratoga half an hour before I was arrested in the public house in Montpelier and taken before a magistrate, on complaint of Miss Bradley, of Rutland, that I was guilty of bigamy.

The examination was a long one, and as the facts which were then shown appeared afterwards in my trial they need not be noted now. I had two first- rate lawyers, but for all that, and with the plainest showing that Margaret Bradley had no claim whatever to be considered my wife, I was bound over in the sum of three thousand dollars to appear for trial, and was sent to jail. There was a tremendous excitement about the matter, and the whole town seemed interested.

To jail I went, Eliza going with me, and insisting upon staying; but the jailer would not let her, nor was she permitted to visit me during my entire stay there, at least she got in to see me but once. I made every effort to get bail, but was unsuccessful. Eight long weary months elapsed before my trial came on, and all this while I was in jail. My trial lasted a week. The Bradley woman knew she was no more married to me than she was to the man in the moon; but she swore stoutly that we were actually wedded according to the certificate. On the other hand, my son swore to all the facts about the Troy spree, and his buying and filling out the certificate, which showed for itself that, excepting the signature of the young woman who also witnessed it, it was entirely in Henry's handwriting. I should have got along well enough so far as the Bradley woman was concerned; but the prosecution had been put in possession of all the facts relative to my first and worst marriage, and the whole matter came up in this case. The District Attorney had sent everywhere, as far even as Illinois, for witness with regard to that marriage. It seemed as if all Vermont was against me. I have heard that with the cost of witnesses and other expenses, my trial cost the state more than five thousand dollars. My three lawyers could not save me. After a week's trial the case went to the jury, and in four hours they returned a verdict of "guilty."

My counsel instantly appealed the case to the Supreme Court, and, meanwhile I went back to jail where I remained three months more. A few days after I returned to jail a friend of mine managed to furnish me with files and saws, and I went industriously to work at the gratings of my window to saw my way out. I could work only at night, when the keepers were away, and I covered the traces of my cuttings by filling in with tallow. In two months I had everything in readiness for my escape. An hour's more sawing at the bars would set me free. But just at that time the Governor of the State, Fletcher, made a visit to the jail. I told him all about my case. He assured me, after hearing all the circumstances, that if I should be convicted and sentenced, he would surely pardon me in the course of six or eight weeks. Trusting in this promise, I made no further effort to escape though I could have done so easily any night; but rather than run the risk of recapture, and a heavier sentence if I should be convicted, I awaited the chances of the court, and looked beyond for the clemency of the Governor.

Well, finally my case came up in the Supreme Court. It only occupied a day, and the result was that I was sentenced for three years in the State prison. I was remanded to jail, and five days from that time I was taken from Montpelier to Windsor.

CHAPTER X.

PRISON-LIFE IN VERMONT.

ENTERING PRISON - THE SCYTHE SNATH BUSINESS -
BLISTERED HANDS - I LEARN NOTHING - THREAT TO
KILL THE SHOP - KEEPER - LOCKSMITHING - OPEN
REBELLION - SIX WEEKS IN THE DUNGEON - ESCAPE OF
A PRISONER - IN THE DUNGEON AGAIN - THE MAD
MAN, HALL - HE ATTEMPTS TO MURDER THE DEPUTY -
I SAVE MOREY'S LIFE - HOWLING IN THE BLACK HOLE -
TAKING OFF HALL'S IRONS - A GHASTLY SPECTACLE -
A PRISON FUNERAL - I AM LET ALONE - BETTER
TREATMENT - THE FULL TERM OF MY IMPRISONMENT.

We arrived at Windsor and I was safely inside of the
prison at three o'clock in the afternoon. Warden
Harlow met me with a joke, to the effect that, had it
not been for my handcuffs he should have taken the
officer who brought me, to be the prisoner, I was so
much the better dressed of the two. He then talked very
seriously to me for a long time. He was sorry, and
surprised, he said, to see a man of my appearance
brought to such a place for such a crime; he could not
understand how a person of my evident intelligence
should get into such a scrape.

I told him that he understood it as well as I did, at all
events; that I could not conceive why I should get into
these difficulties, one after the other; but that I

believed I was a crazy man on this one subject-matrimonial monomania; that when I had gone through with one of these scrapes, and had suffered the severe punishment that was almost certain to follow, the whole was like a dream to me - a nightmare and nothing more. With regard to what was before me in this prison I should try and behave myself, and make the best of the situation; but I notified the Warden that I did not mean to do one bit of work if I could help it.

He took me inside, where my fine clothes were taken away, and I. was dressed in the usual particolored prison uniform. I was told the rules, and was warned that if I did not observe them it would go hard with me. Then followed twenty-four hours solitary confinement, and the next afternoon I was taken from my cell to a shop in which scythe snaths were made.

It had transpired during my trial at Montpelier, that when I was a young man, I was a blacksmith by trade. This information had been transmitted to prison and I was at once put to work making heel rings. It was some years since I had worked at a forge and handled a hammer. Consequently, in three or four days, my hands were terribly blistered, and as the Warden happened to come into the shop, I showed them to him, and quietly told him that I would do that work no longer. He told me that I must do it; he would make me do it. I answered that he might kill me, or punish me in any way he pleased, but he could not make me do that kind of labor, and I threw down my hammer and refused to work a moment longer.

The Warden left me and sent Deputy Warden Morey to try me. He approached me in a kindly way, and I showed my blistered hands to him. He thought that was the way to "toughen" me. I thought not, and said so, and, moreover, told him I would never make another heel ring in that prison, and I never did.

He sent me to my cell and I stayed there a week, till my hands were well. Then the Deputy came to me and asked me if I was willing to learn to hew out scythe snaths in the rough for the shavers, who finished them? I said I would try. I went into the shop and was shown how the work was to be done. Every man was expected to hew out fifty snaths in a day. In three or four days the shop-keeper came and overlooked me while I was working in my bungling way, and said if I couldn't do better than that I must clear out of his shop and do something else. My reply was that I did not understand the business, and had no desire or intention to learn it. He sent for the Deputy Warden, who came and expressed the opinion that I could not do anything. I said I was willing to do anything I could understand.

"Do you understand anything?" asked the Deputy.

Well, some things, marrying for instance," was my answer.

"I want no joking or blackguardism about this matter," said the Deputy; "them simple fact is, you've got to work; if you don't we'll make you."

So I kept on at hewing, making no improvement, and in a day or two more the shopkeeper undertook to show me how the work should be done. I protested I never could learn it.

"You don't try; and I have a good mind to punish you."

The moment the shop-keeper said it I dropped the snath, raised my axe, and told him that if he came one step nearer to me I would make mincemeat of him. He thought it was advisable to stay where he was; but one of the prison-keepers was in the shop, and as he came toward me I warned him that he had better keep away.

All the men in the shop were ready to break out in insubordination; when I threatened the shop keeper and the guard, they cheered; the Deputy Warden was soon on the ground; he stood in the doorway a moment, and then, in a kind tone called me to him. I had no immediate quarrel with him, and so I dropped my axe and went to him. He told me that there was no use of "making a muss" there, it incited the other prisoners to insubordination, and was sure to bring severe punishment upon myself. "Go and get your cap and coat," said he "and come with me."

"But if you are going to put me into that black hole of yours," I exclaimed, "I won't go; you'll have to draw me there or kill me on the way."

He promised he would not put me in the dungeon, he was only going to put me in my cell, he said, and to my cell I went, willingly enough, and stayed there a week, during which time I suppose everyone of my shop-mates thought I was in the dungeon, undergoing severe punishment for my rebellions conduct.

I had learned now the worst lesson which a pris- oner can learn-that is, that my keepers were afraid of me. To a limited extent, it is true, I was now my own master and keeper. In a few days Deputy Morey came to me and asked me if I was "willing" to come out and work. I was sick of solitary confinement, and longed to see the faces of men, even prisoners: so I told him if I could get any work I could do I was willing to try it, and would do as well as I knew how. He asked me if I knew anything of locksmithing? I told him I had some taste for it, and if he would show me his job I would let him see what I could do.

The fact is, I was a very fair amateur locksmith, and had quite a fondness for fixing, picking, and fussing generally over locks. Accordingly, when he gave me a lock to work upon to make it "play easier," as he described it, I did the job so satisfactorily that I had nearly every lock in the prison to take off and operate upon, if it was nothing more than to clean and oil one. This business occupied my entire time and attention for nearly three months. Then I repaired iron bedsteads, did other iron work, and I was the general tinker of the prison.

It came into my head, however, one day, that I might as well do nothing. The prison fare was indescribably bad, almost as bad as the jail fare at Easton. We lived upon the poorest possible salt beef for dinner, varied now and then with plucks and such stuff from the slaughter houses, with nothing but bread and rye coffee for breakfast and supper, and mush and molasses perhaps twice a week.

I was daily abused, too, by the Warden, his Deputy, and his keepers. They looked upon me as an ugly, insubordinate, refractory, rebellious rascal, who was ready to kill any of them, and, worst of all, who would not work. I determined to confirm their minds in the latter supposition, and so one day I threw down my tools and refused to do another thing.

They dragged me to the dungeon and thrust me in. It was a wretched dark hole, with a little dirty straw in one corner to lie upon. My entire food and drink was bread and water. The man who brought it never spoke to me. His face was the only one I saw during the livelong day. Day and night were alike to me; I lost the run of time; but at long intervals, once in eight or ten days, I suppose, the Deputy came to this hole and asked me if I would come out and work.

"No, no!" I always answered, "never!" Then I paced the stone floor in the dark, or lay on my straw. I lay there till my hips were worn raw. No human being can conceive the agony, the suffering endured in this dungeon. At last I was nearly blind, and was scarcely able to stand up. I presume that the attendant who brought my daily dole of bread and my cup of water, reported my condition. One day the door opened and I was ordered out. They were obliged to bring me out; I was so reduced that I was but the shadow of myself. They meant to cure my obstinacy or to kill me, and had not quite succeeded in doing either.

There was no use in asking me if I would go to work then; I was just alive. A few days in my own cell, in the daylight, and with something beside bread and water to eat, partially restored me. I was then taken into the shop where the snaths were finished by scraping and varnishing, the lightest part of the work, but I would not learn, would not do, would not try to do anything at all. They gave me up. The whole struggle nearly killed me, but I beat them. I was turned into the halls and told to do what I could, which, I knew well enough, meant what I would.

After that I worked about the halls and yard,

sometimes sweeping, and again carrying something, or doing errands for the keepers from one part of the prison to another. I was what theatrical managers call a general utility man, and, not at all strangely, for it is human nature, now that I could do what I pleased, I pleased to do a great deal, and was tolerably useful, and far more agreeable than I had been in the past.

There was a young fellow, twenty-two years of age, in one of the cells, serving out a sentence of six years. When I was sweeping around I used to stop and talk to him every day. One day he was missing. He had been supposed to be sick or asleep for several hours, for apparently lie lay in bed, and was lying very still. But that was only an ingeniously constructed dummy. The young man himself had made a hole under his bed into an adjoining vacant cell, the door of which stood open. He had crawled through his hole, come out of the vacant cell door, and gone up to the prison garret, where he found some old pieces of rope. These he tied together, and getting out at the cupola upon the roof, he managed to let himself down on the outside of the building and got away. He was never recaptured. The Warden said that some one must have told him about the adjoining vacant cell, with its always open door, else how would the young man have known it?

I was accused of imparting this valuable information, and I suffered four weeks' confinement in that horrible dungeon on the mere suspicion. This made ten weeks in all of my prison-life in a hole in which I suffered so that I hoped I should die there.

One of the prisoners was a desperate man, named Hall. He was a convicted murderer, and was sentenced for life. He too, worked about in the prison and the yards, dragging or carrying a heavy ball and chain. When bundles of snaths were to be carried from one shop to the other in the various processes of finishing, Hall had to do it, and to carry his ball and chain as well, so that he was loaded like a pack-horse. No pack-horse was ever so abused.

Of course he was ugly; the wardens and the keepers knew it, and generally kept away from him.

I talked with him more than once, and he told me that with better treatment he should be a better man. "Look at the loads which are put on me every day," he would say; as if this ball and chain were not as much as I can carry; and this for life, for life!

One day when Hall and I were working together in the prison, Deputy Warden Morey came in and said something to him, and in a moment the man sprung upon him. He had secured somehow, perhaps he had picked it up in the yard, a pocket knife, and with this he stabbed the Warden, striking him in the shoulder, arm, and where he could.

Morey was a man sixty-five years of age, and he made such resistance as he could, crying out loudly for help. I turned, ran to Hall, and with one blow of my fist knocked him nearly senseless; then help came and we secured the mad man. Morey was profuse in protestations of gratitude to me for saving his life.

There was a great excitement over this attempt to murder the Deputy, and for a few hours, with wardens and keepers, I was a hero. I had been in the prison more than a year, and was generally regarded as one of the worst prisoners, one of the "hardest cases;" a mere chance had suddenly made me one of the most commendable men within those dreary walls. As for Hall, he was taken to the dungeon and securely chained by the feet to a ring in the center of the stone floor. There is no doubt whatever that the man was a raving maniac. He howled night and day so that he could be heard everywhere in the prison-"Murder, murder! they are murdering me in this black hole; why don't they take me out and kill me?"

The Warden said it could not be helped; that the man must be kept there; he was dangerous to himself and others; the dark cell was the only place for him. So Hall stayed there and howled, his cries growing weaker from day to day; by-and-by we heard him only at intervals, and after that not at all.

One morning there was a little knot of men around the open dungeon door, the Deputy Warden and two or three keepers. Mr. Morey called to me to go and get the tools and come there and take off Hall's irons. I went into the cell and in a few minutes I unfastened his feet from the ring; then I took the shackles off his limbs. I thought he held his legs very stiff, but knew he was obstinate, and only wondered he was so quiet.

Somebody brought in a candle and I looked at Hall's face. I never saw a more ghastly sight. The blood from his mouth and nostrils had clotted on the lower part of his face, and his wild eyes, fixed and glassy, were staring at the top wall of the dungeon. He must have been dead several hours. The Depu ty and the rest knew he was dead-the man who carried in the bread and water told them-me it came with a shock from which I did not soon recover.

They buried Hall in the little graveyard which was in the yard of the prison. An Episcopal clergyman, who was chaplain of the prison, read the burial service over him. The prisoners were brought out to attend the homely funeral. The ball and chain, all the personal property left by Hall, were put aside for the next murderer sentenced for life, or for the next "ugly" prisoner. "If I were only treated better, and not abused so, I should be a better man." This is what Hall used to say to me whenever he had an opportunity. The last and worst and best in that prison had been done for him now.

From the day when I rescued Morey from the hands of Hall, his whole manner changed towards me, and he treated me with great kindness, frequently bringing me a cup of tea or coffee, and something good to eat. He also promised to present the circumstances of the Hall affair to the Governor, and to urge my pardon, but I do not think he ever did so, at least I heard nothing of it. When I pressed the matter upon Morey's attention he said it would do no good till I had served out half my sentence, and then he would see what could be done.

I served half my sentence, and then the other half, every day of it. But during the last two years I had very little to complain of except the loss of my liberty. I was put into the cook shop where I could get better food, and I did pretty much what I pleased. By general consent I was let alone. They had found out that ill usage only made me "ugly," while kindness made me at least behave myself. And so the three weary years of my confinement were on to an end.

CHAPTER XI.

ON THE TRAMP.

THE DAY OF MY DELIVERANCE - OUT OF CLOTHES - SHARING WITH A BEGGAR-A GOOD FRIEND - TRAMPING THROUGH THE SNOW - WEARY WALKS - TRUSTING TO LUCK - COMFORT AT CONCORD - AT MEREDITH BRIDGE - THE BLAISDELLS - LAST OF THE "BLOSSOM" BUSINESS - MAKING MONEY AT PORTSMOUTH - REVISITING WINDSOR - AN ASTONISHED WARDEN - MAKING FRIENDS OF OLD ENEMIES - INSPECTING THE PRISON - GOING TO PORT JERVIS.

At last the happy day of my deliverance came. The penalty for pretending to marry one milliner and for being married by another milliner was paid. My sentence was fulfilled. I had looked forward to this day for months. Of all my jail and prison life in different States, this in Vermont was the hardest, the most severe. My obstinacy, no doubt, did much at first to enhance my sufferings, and it was the accident only of my saving Morey's life that made the last part of my imprisonment a little more tolerable. When I was preparing to go, it was discovered that the fine suit of clothes I wore into the prison had been given by mistake or design to some one else, and my silk hat and calf-skin boots had gone with the clothes. But never mind! I would have gone out into the world in rags-my liberty was all I wanted then. The Warden gave me one of his own old coats, a ragged pair of pantaloons, and a new pair of brogan shoes. He also gave me three dollars, which was precisely a dollar a year for my services, and this was more than I ever meant to earn there. Thus equipped and supplied I was sent out into the streets of Windsor.

I had not gone half a mile before I met a poor old woman whom I had known very well in Rutland. She recognized me at once, though I know I was sadly changed for the worse. She was on her way to Fall River, where she had relatives, and where she hoped for help, but had no money to pay her fare, so I divided my small stock with her, and that left me just one dollar and a half with which to begin the world again. I went down to the bridge and the toll-gatherer gave me as much as I could eat, twenty five cents in money, and a pocket-full of food to carry with me. I was heading, footing rather, for Meredith Bridge in New Hampshire. It was in the month of December; and I was poorly clad and with- out an overcoat. I must have walked fifteen miles that afternoon, and just at nightfall I came to a wayside public house and ventured to go in. As I stood by the fire, the landlord stepped up and slapping me on the shoulder, said:

"Friend, you look as if you were in trouble; step up and have something to drink."

I gladly accepted the invitation to partake of the first glass of liquor I had tasted in three years. It was something, too, everything to be addressed thus kindly. I told this worthy landlord my whole story; how I had been trapped by the two milliners, and how I had subsequently suffered. He had read something about it in the papers; he felt as if he knew me; he certainly was sorry for me; and he proved his sympathy by giving me what then seemed to me the best supper I had ever eaten, a good bed, a good breakfast, a package of provisions to carry with me, and then sent me on my way with a comparatively light heart.

It rained, snowed, and drizzled all day long. I tramped through the wet snow ankle deep, but made nearly forty miles before night, and then came to a public house which I knew well. When I was in the bar-room drying myself and warming my wet and half-frozen feet, I could not but think how, only a few years before, I had put up at that very house, with a fine horse and buggy of my own in the stable, and plenty of money in my pocket. The landlord's face was familiar enough, but he did not know me, nor, under my changed circumstances, did I desire that he should. Supper, lodging, and breakfast nearly exhausted my small money capital; I was worn and weary, too, and the next day was able to walk but twenty miles, all told. On the way, at noon I went into a farm house to warm myself. The woman had just baked a short-cake which stood on the hearth, toward which I must have cast longing eyes, for the farmer said:

"Have you had your dinner, man?"

"No, and I have no money to buy any."

"Well, you don't need money here. Wife, put that short-cake and some butter on the table; now, my man, fall to and eat as much as you like."

I was very hungry, and I declare I ate the whole of that short-cake. I told these people that I had been in better circumstances, and that I was not always the poor, ragged, hungry wretch I appeared then. They made we welcome to what I had eaten and when I went away filled my pockets with food. At night I was about thirty miles above Concord. I had no money, but trusting to luck, I got on the cars-the conductor came, and when he found I had no ticket, he said he must put me off. It was a bitter night and I told him I should be sure to freeze to death. A gentleman who heard the conversation at once paid my fare, for which I expressed my grateful thanks, and I went to Concord.

On my arrival I went to a hotel and told the landlord I wanted to stay there till the next day, when a conductor whom I knew would be going to Meredith Bridge; that I was going with him, and that he would probably pay my bill at the hotel. "All right," said the landlord, and he gave me my supper and a room. The next noon my friend, the conductor, came and when I first spoke to him he did not recognize me; I told him who I was, but to ask me no questions as to how I came to appear in those old clothes, and to be so poor; I wanted to borrow five dollars, and to go with him to Meredith Bridge. He greeted me very cordially, handed me a ten-dollar Bill-twice as much as I asked for-said he was not going to the Bridge till next day, and told me meanwhile, to go to the hotel and make myself comfortable.

I went back to the hotel, paid my bill, stayed there that day and night, and the next morning "deadheaded," with my friend the conductor to Meredith Bridge. Everybody knew me there. The hotel-keeper made me welcome to his house, and said I could stay as long as I liked.

"Say, dew ye ever cure anybody, Doctor?" asked my old friend, the landlord, and he laughed and nudged me in the ribs, and asked me to take some of his medicine from the bar, which I immediately did.

I was at home now. But the object of my visit was to see if I could not collect some of my old bills in that neighborhood, amounting in the aggregate to several hundred dollars. They were indeed old bills of five or six years' standing, and I had very little hope of collecting much money. I went first to Lake Village, and called on Mr. John Blaisdell, the husband of the woman whom I had cured of the dropsy, in accordance, as she believed at the time, with her prophetic dream. Blaisdell didn't know me at first; then he wanted to know what my bill was; I told him one hundred dollars, to say nothing of six years' interest; he said he had no money, though he was regarded as a rich man, and in fact was.

"But sir," said I, "you see me and how poor I am. Give me something on account. I am so poor that I even borrowed this overcoat from the tailor in the village, that I might present a little more respectable appearance when I called on my old patients to try to collect some of my old bills. Please to give me something."

But he had no money. He would pay for the overcoat; I might tell the tailor so; and afterwards he gave me a pair of boots and an old shirt. This was the fruit which my "blossom" of years before brought at last. I saw Mrs. Blaisdell, but she said she could do nothing for me. She had forgotten what I had done for her.

Of all my bills in that vicinity, with a week's dunning, I collected only three dollars; but a good friend of mine,

Sheriff Hill, went around and succeeded in making up a purse of twenty dollars which he put into my hands just as I was going away. My old landlord wanted nothing for my week's board; all he wanted was to know "if I ever cured anybody;" and when I told him I did, "sometimes" he insisted upon my taking more of his medicine, and he put up a good bottle of it for me to carry with me on my journey.

With my twenty dollars I went to Portsmouth, where I speedily felt that I was among old and true friends. I had not been there a day before I was called upon to take care of a young man who was sick, and after a few weeks charge of him I received in addition to my board and expenses, three hundred dollars. I was now enabled to clothe myself handsomely, and I did so and went to Newburyport, where I remained several weeks and made a great deal of money.

In the spring I went to White River Junction, and while I was in the hotel taking a drink with some friends, who should come into the bar-room but the Lake Village tailor from whom I had borrowed the overcoat which I had even then on my back. I was about to thank him for his kindness to me when he took me aside and said reproachfully:

"Doctor, you wore away my overcoat and this is it, I think."

"Good heavens! didn't John Blaisdell pay you for the coat? He told me he would; its little enough out of what he owes me."

"He never said a word to me about it," was the reply. I told the tailor the circumstances; I did not like to let him to know that I had then about seven hundred dollars in my pocket; I wished to appear poor as long as there was a chance to collect any of my Meredith and Lake Village bills; so I offered him three dollars to take back the coat. He willingly consented and that was the last of the "Blossom" business with the Blaisdells.

I was bound not to leave this part of the country without revisiting Windsor, and I went there, stopping at the best house in the town, and, I fear, "putting on airs" a little. I had suffered so much in this place that I wanted to see if there was any enjoyment to be had there. Satisfaction there was, certainly-the satisfaction one feels in going back under the most favorable circumstances, to a spot where he has endured the very depths of misery. After a good dinner I set out to visit the prison. Here was the very spot in the street where, only a few months before, I, a ragged beggar, had divided my mere morsel of money with the poor woman from Rutland. What change in my circumstances those few months had wrought. I had recovered my health which bad food, ill usage, and imprisonment had broken down, and was in the best physical condition. The warden's old coat and pantaloons had been exchanged for the finest clothes that money would buy. I had a good gold watch and several hundred dollars in my pocket. I had seen many of my old friends, and knew that they were still my friends, and I was fully restored to my old position. My three years' imprisonment was only a blank in my existence; I had begun life again and afresh, precisely where I left off before I fell into the hands of the two Vermont milliners.

All this was very pleasant to reflect upon; but do not

believe I thought even then, that the reason for this change in my circumstances, and changes for the better, was simply because I had minded my business and had let women alone.

When I called on Warden Harlow, and courteously asked to be shown about the prison, he got up and was ready to comply with my request, when he looked me full in the face and started back in amazement:

"Well, I declare! Is this you?"

"Yes, Warden Harlow; but I want you to understand that while I am here I do not intend to do a bit of work, and you can't make me. You may as well give it up first as last; I won't work anyhow."

The Warden laughed heartily, and sent for Deputy Morey who came in to "see a gentleman," and was much astonished to find the prisoner, who, two years before, had saved his life from the hands and knife of the madman Hall. I spent a very pleasant hour with my old enemies, and I took occasion to give them a hint or two with regard to the proper treatment of prisoners. I then made the rounds of the prison, and went into the dungeon where I had passed so many wretched hours for weeks at a time. The warden and his deputy congratulated me upon my improved appearance and prospects, and hoped that my whole future career would be equally prosperous.

Nor did I forget to call up my friend in need and friend indeed in the toll-house at the bridge. I stayed three or four days in Windsor, finding it really a charming place, and I was almost sorry to leave it. But my only purpose in going there, that is to revisit the prison, was accomplished, and I started for New York, and went from there to Port Jervis, where I met my eldest son.

CHAPTER XII.

ATTEMPT TO KIDNAP SARAH SCHEIMER'S BOY.

STARTING TO SEE SARAH - THE LONG SEPARATION - WHAT I LEARNED ABOUT HER - HER DRUNKEN HUSBAND - CHANGE OF PLAN - A SUDDENLY - FORMED SCHEME - I FIND SARAH'S SON - THE FIRST INTERVIEW - RESOLVE TO KIDNAP THE BOY - REMONSTRANCES OF MY SON HENRY - THE ATTEMPT - A DESPERATE STRUGGLE - THE RESCUE - ARREST OF HENRY - MY FLIGHT INTO PENNSYLVANIA - SENDING ASSISTANCE TO MY SON - RETURN TO PORT JERVIS - BAILING HENRY - HIS RETURN TO BELVIDERE - HE IS BOUND OVER TO BE TRIED FOR KIDNAPPING - MY FOLLY.

After I had been in Port Jervis three or four days I matured a plan that had long been forcing in my mind, and that was, to try and see Sarah Scheimer once more, or at least to find out something about her and about our son. The boy, if he was living, must be about ten years of age. I had never seen him; nor, since the night when I was taken out of bed and carried to the Easton jail had I ever seen Sarah, or even heard from her, except by the message the Methodist minister brought to me from her the day after I was released from jail. In the long interval I had married the Newark widow, and had served a brief term in the New Jersey State prison for doing it; I had married Mary Gordon, in New

Hampshire, and had run away, not only from her, but from constables and the prison in that state; the mock marriage with the Rutland woman at Troy, and the altogether too real marriage with the Montpelier milliner had followed; I had spent three wretched years in the Vermont prison at Windsor; and numerous other exciting adventures had checkered my career. What had happened to Sarah and her son during all this while? There was not a week in the whole time since our sudden separation when I had not thought of Sarah; and now I was near her old home, with means at my command, leisure on my hands, and I was determined to know something about her and the child.

So long a time had elapsed and I was so changed in my personal appearance that I had little fear of being recognized by any one in Pennsylvania or the adjoining part of New Jersey, who would molest me. The old matters must have been pretty much forgotten by all but the very few who were immediately interested in them. It was safe to make the venture at all events, and, I resolved to make the venture to see and learn what I could.

I had the idea in my mind that if Sarah was alive and well, and free, I should be able to induce her to fulfil her promise to come to me, and that we might go somewhere and settle down and live happily together. At any rate, I would try to see her and our child.

I did not communicate a word of all this to my son Henry. I told him I was going to New Jersey to visit some friends, to look for business, and I would like to have him accompany me. He consented; I hired a horse and carriage, and one bright morning we started. I had no friends to visit, no business to do, except to see

Sarah-the dearest and best-loved of all my wives.

When we reached Water Gap I found an old acquaintance in the landlord of the hotel, and I told him where I was going, and what I hoped to do. He knew the Scheimers, knew all that had happened eleven years before, and he told me that Sarah had married again, seven years ago, and was the mother of two more children. She lived on a farm, half a mile from Oxford, and her husband who had married her for her money, and had been urged upon her by her parents, was a shiftless, worthless, drunken fellow. The boy-my boy-was alive and well, and was with his mother.

This intelligence changed, or rather made definite my plan. Sarah was nothing to me now. The boy was everything. I must see him, and if he was what he was represented to be, a bright little fellow, I determined that he should no longer remain in the hands and under the control of his drunken step-father, but I would carry him away with me if I could. It was nearly noon when we arrived at Oxford, and going to my old quarters, I found that "Boston Yankee," had long since left the place. There was a new landlord, and I saw no familiar faces about the house; all was new and strange to me. I made inquiries, and soon found out that Sarah's boy went to a school in town not far from the hotel, and I went there to "prospect," leaving Henry at the public house.

It was noon now, and fifty or more boys were trooping out of school. I carefully scanned the throng. The old proverb has it that it is a wise child who knows its own father; but it is not so difficult for a father to know his own children. The moment I put my eyes on Sarah's son, I knew him; he was the very image of me; I could have picked him out of a thousand. I beckoned to the boy and he came to me. He was barefoot; and his very toes betrayed him, for they "overrode" just as mine did; but his face was enough and would have been evidence of his identity as my son in any court in Christendom.

"Do you know me, my little man?" said I.

"No, sir, I do not."

"Do you know what was your mother's name before she was married?"

"Yes Sir, it was Sarah Scheimer."

"Do you know that the man with whom you live is not your rather?"

"Oh, yes, Sir, I know that; mother always told me so; but she never told me who my father was."

"My son," said I taking him in my arms, "I am your father; wait about here a few minutes till I can go and get my horse and carriage, and I will take you to ride."

I ran over to the hotel; ordered my horse to be brought to the door at once, got into the wagon with Henry and told him that Sarah Scheimer's boy was just across the way, and that I was going to carry him off with us. Henry implored me not to do it, and said it was dangerous. I never stopped to think of danger when my will impelled me. I did not know that at that moment, men who had noticed my excited manner, and who knew I was "up to something," were watching me from the hotel piazza. I drove over where the boy was waiting, called him to me, and Henry held the reins while I put out my hands to pull the boy into the carriage. Two of the men who were watching me came at once, one of them taking the horse by the head, and the other coming to me and demanding:

"What are you going to do with that boy?"

"Take him with me; he is my son."

"No you don't," said the man, and he laid hold of the boy and attempted to pull him out of the wagon. I also seized the lad who began to scream. In the struggle for possession, I caught up the whip and struck the man with the handle, felling him to the ground. All the while the other man was shouting for assistance. The crowd gathered. The boy was roughly torn from me, in spite of my efforts to retain him. Henry was thoroughly alarmed; and while the mob were trying to pull us also out of the carriage he whipped the horse till he sprang through the crowd and was well off in a moment.

"Get out of town as fast as you can drive," said I to Henry.

We were not half an hour in reaching Belvidere. There I stopped to breathe the horse a few minutes, and Henry insisted that he was starving, and must have something to eat; he would go into the hotel he said, and get some dinner. I told him it was madness to do it; but he would not move an inch further on the road till he had some dinner. He went into the dining room, and I paced up and down the piazza, nervous, anxious, fearing pursuit, dreading capture, well knowing what would happen when those Jerseymen should get hold of me and find out who I was. At that moment I saw the pursuers coming rapidly up the road. I called to my son:

"Henry, Henry! for God's sake come out here, quick!"

But he thought I was only trying to frighten him so as to hurry him away from his dinner, and get him on the road, and he paid no attention to my summons. I knew that I was the man who was wanted, and, without waiting for Henry, I jumped into my wagon and drove off. I just escaped, that's all. The moment I left, my pursuers were at the door. I looked back and saw them drag my son out of the house, and take him away with them. I turned my horse's head towards the Belvidere Bridge. All the country about there was as familiar to me as the county I was born in. I knew every road, and I had no fear of being caught. Once across the bridge and in Pennsylvania, and I was comparatively safe, unless I myself should be kidnapped as I was at midnight, only a little way from this very spot, eleven years before. Here was an opportunity now to rest and reflect. Confound those Scheimers and all their blood! Was I never to see the end of the scrapes that family would get me into, or which I was to get myself into, on account of the Scheimers?

Surely they could not harm Henry. They might have taken him merely in the hope of drawing me back to try to clear him, or rescue him, and then they would get hold of the man they wanted. My son had done nothing. He did not even know of the contemplated abduction till five minutes before it was attempted, and then he protested against it. He only held the horse when I pulled the lad into the wagon.

Nothing showed so completely the consciousness of

his own entire innocence in the matter, as the coolness with which he sat down to his dinner in Belvidere, and insisted upon remaining when I warned him of our danger. These facts shown, any magistrate before whom he might be taken, must let him go at once. I thought, perhaps, if I waited a few hours where I was, he would be sure to rejoin me, and we could then return to Port Jervis without Sarah's son to be sure; but, otherwise, no worse off than we were when we set out on this ill-starred expedition in the morning.

All this seemed so plain to me that I sent over to Belvidere for a lawyer, who soon came across the bridge to see me, and to him I narrated the whole circumstances of the case from, beginning to end. I asked him if I had not a right to carry off the boy whom I knew to be my own? His reply was that he would not stop to discuss that question; all he knew was that there was a great hue and cry after me for kidnapping the boy; that my son was seized and held for aiding and abetting in the attempted abduction; and he advised me, as a friend, to leave that part of the country as soon as possible. I gave him fifty dollars to look after Henry's case. He thought, considering how little, and that little involuntarily, my son had to do with the matter, be might be got off; he would do all he could for him anyhow. He then returned to Belvidere, and I took the road north.

When I arrived at Port Jervis I detailed to my landlord the whole occurences of the day- what I had tried to do, and how miserably I had failed, and asked him what was to be done next. He said "nothing;" we could only wait and see what happened.

The day following I received a letter from the

Belvidere lawyer informing me that Henry had been examined, had been bound over in the sum of three hundred dollars to take his trial on a charge of kidnapping, and he was then in the county jail. I at once showed this letter to the landlord, and he offered to go down with another man to Belvidere and see about the bail. I gave him three hundred dollars, which be took with him and put into the bands of a resident there who became bail, and in a day or two Henry came back with them to Port Jervis.

My son was frantic; he had been roughly treated; and to think, he said, that he should be thrust into the common jail and kept there two days with all sorts of scoundrels, when he had done actually nothing! He would go back there, stand his trial, and prove his innocence, if he died for it. He reproached me for attempting to carry off the boy against his advice and warning; he knew we should into trouble; but he would show them that he had nothing to do with it; that's what he would do.

Now this was precisely what I did not wish to have him do. A trial of this case, even if Henry should come off scott free, would be certain to revive the whole of the old Scheimer story, which had nearly died away, and which I had no desire to have brought before the public again in any way whatever. The bail bond I was willing, eager even to forfeit, if that would end the matter. But Henry was sure they couldn't touch him, and he meant to have the three hundred dollars returned to me.

Seeing how sensitive the boy was on the subject, and how bent he was on proving his innocence, I thought it best to draw him away from the immediate locality, and so, in the course of a week, I persuaded him to go to New York with me, and we afterward went to Maine for a few weeks to sell my medicines. This Maine trip was a most lucrative one, which was very fortunate, for the money I made there, to the amount of several hundred dollars, was shortly needed for purposes which I did not anticipate when I put the money by.

We returned to New York, and I supposed that Henry had given up all idea of attempting to "prove his innocence;" indeed we had no conversation about the kidnapping affair for several weeks. But he slipped away from me. One day I came back to the hotel, and, inquiring for him, was told at the office he had left word for me that he had gone to Belvidere. A letter from him a day or two afterward confirmed this, to me, unhappy intelligence. The time was near at hand for his trial, and he had gone and given himself up to the authorities. He wrote to me again that he had sent word about his situation to his mother-my first and worst wife-and she and his sister were already with him.

Of course it was impossible for me to go there, if there were no other reasons, I was too immediately interested in this affair to be present, and I had no idea of undergoing a trial and a certain conviction for myself. But I sent down a New York lawyer with one hundred dollars, directing him to employ council there, and to advise and assist as much as he could. Meanwhile, I remained in New York, anxious, it is true, yet almost certain that it would be impossible, under the circumstances, to convict Henry of the kidnapping for which he was indicted. He had not even assisted in the affair, and was sure his counsel would be able to so convince the court and jury.

And reviewing the whole matter, now in my cooler moments, this scheme of trying to carry away Sarah's son, seemed to be as foolish, useless, and mad, as any one of my marrying adventures. Till I picked him out from among his schoolmates, I had never seen the child at all. When I started from Port Jervis to go down, as I supposed, into Pennsylvania, I had no more idea of kidnapping the boy than I had of robbing a sheep-fold. It was only when the landlord at Water Gap told me that Sarah had remarried, and was wedded to a worthless, drunken husband, that I conceived the plan of removing the boy from such associations. I was going to bring him up in a respectable manner. Alas! I did not succeed even in bringing him away.

CHAPTER XIII.

ANOTHER WIDOW.

WAITING FOR THE VERDICT - MY SON SENT TO STATE PRISON - WHAT SARAH WOULD HAVE DONE - INTERVIEW WITH MY FIRST WIFE - HELP FOR HENRY - THE BIDDEFORD WIDOW - HER EFFORT TO MARRY ME - OUR VISIT TO BOSTON - A WARNING - A GENEROUS GIFT - HENRY PARDONED - CLOSE OF THE SCHEIMER ACCOUNT - VISIT TO ONTARIO COUNTY - MY RICH COUSINS - WHAT MIGHT HAVE BEEN - MY BIRTH-PLACE REVISITED.

I waited with nervous impatience for the close of the trial in New Jersey, when I hoped to welcome my son Henry to New York. It was so plain a case, as it seemed to me, and must appear, I thought, to everybody, that I hardly doubted his instant acquittal. But very shortly the New York lawyer whom I had sent to Belvidere, came back and brought terrible news. Henry had been tried, and notwithstanding the fairest showing in his favor, he was convicted and sentenced to eighteen months imprisonment at Trenton.

As it appeared, it was I really, and not Henry, who was on trial. The circumstances of the desperate struggle, and my knocking down one of the men with the butt of my whip, were conspicuous in the case. Even the little boy was put on the stand, and was made to testify against his older half-brother. Henry himself was astounded at the result of the trial, and was firmly convinced that instead of "proving his innocence" to Jersey jurymen, he had better have let his innocence go by default. We never even got back again the three hundred dollars which had been put into the hands of the man who went bail for Henry when he was bound over for trial. For us, it was bad business from beginning to end.

Henry wrote a letter to me, that just before his trial, before he had delivered himself up, and while he was still under bail, he had gone to see Sarah Scheimer on the little farm which was bought with her money, and was worked, so far as it was worked at all, by her drunken husband. The family were even poorer than the landlord at Water Gap had reported. Sarah herself was miserable and unhappy. She told Henry, when he informed her who he was, that if I had wanted to see her or her son, I should have been welcome. She would have been very glad to have had me take the boy and clothe him decently; but she could not part with him, and would not have let me take him away; still, I could see him at any time, and as often as I liked, and the boy should grow up to know and to look upon me as his father.

And this, really, was all I desired, all I wanted; and it was all easily within my grasp, ready in fact to be put into my hands, and I had gone ahead in my usual mad, blundering way, acting, not only without advice, but against such advice as came from Henry at the last moment, and had alienated the mother from me, lost the boy, and had sent Henry, who was wholly innocent, to state prison for eighteen months.

The poor fellow was take to Trenton and was put into the prison where I had spent seven months. He was almost crazy when he got there. His mother and sister went with him, and took lodgings in the place so as to be near him, to render him any assistance that might be in their power.

I had been idle now for some weeks in New York, and I went back to Maine, to Biddeford, where I lad a good practice. I picked up a good deal of money, and in two months I returned to New York to make a brief visit, and to see if something could not be done for the release of Henry from prison. At my solicitation a friend of mine wrote to Trenton to Henry's mother to come on to New York, and meet me at the Metropolitan Hotel on a specified day, to transact some business. She came, and we met for the first time in several years. We met now simply on business, and there was no expression of sentiment or feeling on either side. We cared nothing for each other. I commended her for her devotion to Henry, and then told her I believed, if the proper efforts were made, he could be pardoned out of prison. I told her what lawyer and other persons to see, and how to proceed in the matter. I gave her the most minute instructions, and then handed her five hundred dollars with which to fee her lawyer, and to pay her and her daughter's living expenses in Trenton. She was grateful for the money, and was only too glad to go to work for Henry; she would have done it long ago if she had only known what to do. We then parted, and I have never seen the woman, since that day.

This business transacted, I at once returned to my practice at Biddeford. Among my patients was a wealthy widow, "fat, fair, and forty," and I had not attended her long before a warm affection sprung up between us, and in time, when the widow recovered, we began to think we were in love with each other. I confess that I agreed to marry her; but it was to be at some distant day-a very distant day as I intended -for, strange as it may seem, and as it did seem to me, I had at last learned the lesson that I had better let matrimony alone. I had married too many wives, widows, milliners, and what not, already, and had suffered too severely for so doing. I meant that my Vermont imprisonment, the worst of all, should be the last.

So I only "courted" the widow, calling upon her almost every day, and I was received and presented to her acquaintances as her affianced husband. Her family and immediate friends were violently opposed to the match, thereby showing their good sense. I was also informed that they knew something of my previous history, and I was warned that I had better not undertake to marry the widow. Bless their innocent hearts! I had no idea of doing it. I was daily amazed at my own common sense. My memory was active now; all my matrimonial mishaps of the past, with all the consequences, were ever present to my mind, and never more present than when was in the company of the fascinating widow. As for her, the more her relatives opposed the match, the more she was bent upon marrying me. Her family, she, said, were afraid they were going to lose her property, but she would never give them a cent of it, anyhow, and she would marry when and whom she pleased.

Not "when," exactly; because, as she protested she would marry me, I had something to say about it; I had been run away with by a milliner in Vermont, and I had no idea of beings forcibly wedded by a widow in Maine. I pleaded that my business was not sufficiently established; I was liable to be called away from time to time; I had affairs to arrange in New York and elsewhere before I could settle down; and so the happy day was put off to an indefinite future time.

By-and-by I had business in Boston, and the widow declared that she would go with me; she wanted to visit her friend's there and do some shopping; and without making particular mention of her intention to her relatives, she went with me, and we were in Boston together more than two weeks. At the end of that time she returned to Biddeford and notified her friends treat she was married to the doctor, though she had no certificate, not even a Troy one, to show for it.

I deemed it advisable not to go back with her, but went to Worcester for a while. In a few days I went to Biddeford, keeping somewhat close, for I did not care to meet any of the relatives, and at night I called upon the widow. She told me that her family had raised a tremendous fuss about me, and had learned as much as they, and indeed she, wanted to know about my adventures in Vermont and New Hampshire. They had not gone back of that, but that was enough. It was dangerous, she told me, for me to stay there; I was sure to be arrested; I had better get away from the place as soon as possible. We might meet again by-and-by, but unless I wanted to be arrested I must leave, the place that very night. She gave me seven hundred dollars, pressed the money upon me, and I parted from her, returning to Worcester, and going from there to Boston. Besides what the widow bad given me, I had made more than one thousand dollars in Maine, and was comparatively well off.

Then came the joyful intelligence that Henry was released. His mother had worked for him night and day. She bad drawn up a petition, secured a large number of sterling signatures, had gone with her counsel to see the Governor, had presented the petition and all the facts in the case, and the Governor had granted a pardon. Henry served only six months of the eighteen for which he was sentenced, and very soon after I received word that he was free, he came to me in Boston, stayed a few days, and then went home to his mother in Unadilla.

With the release of my son, I considered the Scheimer account closed, and I have never made any effort to see Sarah or our boy since that time.

From Boston I went to Pittsford, Ontario County, N. Y., where I had many friends, who knew nothing about any of my marriages or misfortunes, my arrests or imprisonments. I went visiting merely, and enjoyed myself so much that I stayed there nearly three months, going about the country, and practicing a little among my friends. I was never happier than I was during this time. I was free from prisons, free from my wives, and free from care. As a matrimonial monomaniac I now looked upon myself as cured.

Among the friends whom I visited in Ontario County, and with whom I passed several pleasant weeks, were two cousins of mine whom I had not seen for many years, since we were children in fact, but who gave me a most cordial welcome, and made much of me while I was there. They knew absolutely nothing of my unhappy history-no unpleasant rumor even respecting me, had ever penetrated that quiet quarter of the State. I told them what I pleased of my past career, from boyhood to the present time, and to them I was only a tolerably successful doctor, who made money enough to live decently and dress well, and who was then suffering from overwork and badly in need of recuperation. This, indeed, was the ostensible reason for my visit to Ontario. I was somewhat shattered; my old prison trials and troubles began to tell upon me. I used to think sometimes that I was a little "out of my head;" I certainly was so whenever I entered upon one of my matrimonial schemes, and I must have been as mad as a March hare when I attempted to kidnap Sarah Scheimer's boy. After all the excitement and suffering of the past few years, I needed rest, and here I found it.

My cousins were more than well-to-do farmers; they were enormously rich in lands and money. Just after the war of 1812, their father, my uncle, and my own father, had come to this, then wild and almost uninhabited, section of the State to settle. Soon after they arrived there my father's wife died, and this loss, with the general loneliness of the region, to say nothing of the fever and ague, soon drove my father back to Delaware County to his forge for a living, and to the day of his death he was nothing more than a hard-working, hand-to-mouth-living, common blacksmith.

But my uncle stayed there, and, as time went on, he bought hundreds of acres of land for a mere song, which were now immensely valuable, and had made his children almost the richest people in that region. My Cousins were great farmers, extensive raisers of stock, wool-growers, and everything else that could make them prosperous. There seemed to be no end to their wealth, and their fiat farms, spread out on every side as far as the eye could see.

And if my father had only stayed there, I could not help but think what a different life mine might have been. Instead of being the adventurer I was, and had been ever since I separated from my first and worst wife-doing well, perhaps, for a few weeks or a few months, and then blundering into a mad marriage or other difficulty which got me into prison; well-to-do to-day and to-morrow a beggar - I, too, might have been rich and respectable, and should have, saved myself a world of suffering. This was but a passing thought which did not mar my visit, or make it less pleasant to me. I went there to be happy, not to be miserable, and for three months I was happy indeed.

From there I went to my birthplace in Columbia County, revisiting old scenes and the very few old friends and acquaintances who survived, or who had not moved away. I spent a month there and there-abouts, and at the end of that time I felt full restored to my usual good health, and was ready to go to work again, not in the matrimonial way, but in my medical business, that was enough for me now.

CHAPTER XIV.

MY OWN SON TRIES TO MURDER ME.

SETTLING DOWN IN MAINE - HENRY'S HEALTH - TOUR THROUGH THE SOUTH - SECESSION TIMES - DECEMBER IN NEW ORLEANS - UP THE MISSISSIPPI - LEAVING HENRY IN MASSACHUSETTS - BACK IN MAINE AGAIN - RETURN TO BOSTON - PROFITABLE HORSE TRADING - PLENTY OF MONEY - MY FIRST WIFE'S CHILDREN - HOW THEY HAD BEEN BROUGHT UP - A BAREFACED ROBBERY - ATTEMPT TO BLACKMAIL ME - MY OWN SON TRIES TO ROB AND KILL ME - MY RESCUE - LAST OF THE YOUNG MAN.

Where to go, not what to do, was the next question. Wherever I might go and establish myself, if only for a few days, or a few weeks, I was sure to have almost immediately plenty of patients and customers enough for my medicines-this had been my experience always-and unfortunately for me, I was almost equally sure to get into some difficulty from which escape was not always easy. Looking over the whole ground for a fresh start in business, it seemed to me that Maine was the most favorable place. Whenever I had been there I had done well; it was one of the very few States I had lived in where I had not been in jail or in prison; nor had I been married there, though the Biddeford widow did her best to wed me, and it is not her fault that she did not succeed in doing it.

To Maine, then, I went, settling down in Augusta, and remaining there four months, during which time I had as much as I could possibly attend to, and laid by a very considerable sum of money. While I was there I heard the most unfavorable reports with regard to the health of my eldest son Henry. Prison life at Trenton had broken him down in body as well as in spirit, and he had been ill, some of the time seriously, nearly all the time since he went to Unadilla. The fact that he was entirely innocent of the offence for which he was imprisoned, preyed upon his mind, and with the worst results. As these stories reached me from week to week, I became anxious and even alarmed about him, and at last I left my lucrative business in Augusta and went to New York. I could not well go to Unadilla to visit Henry without seeing his mother, whom I had no desire to see; so I sent for him to come to me in the city if was able to do so. I knew that if medicine or medical attendance would benefit him, I should be able to help him.

In a few days he came to me in a most deplorable physical condition. He was a mere wreck of his former self. Almost immediately he began to talk about the attempt to abduct the boy from Oxford; how innocent he was in the matter, and how terribly he had suffered merely because he happened to be with me when I rashly endeavored to kidnap the lad. All this went through me like a sharp sword. It seemed as if I was the cause, not only of great unhappiness to myself, but of pain and misery to all who were associated or brought in contact with me. For this poor boy, who had endured and suffered so much on my account, I could not do enough. My means and time must now-be devoted to his recovery, if recovery, was possible.

He was weak, but was still able to walk about, and he enjoyed riding very much. I kept him with me in the city a week or two, taking daily rides to the Park and into the country, and when he felt like going out in the evening I made him go to some place of amusement with me. I had no other business, and meant to have none, but to take care of Henry, and I devoted myself wholly to his comfort and happiness. In a few days he had much improved in health and spirits, so much so, that I meditated making a long tour with him to the South, hoping that the journey there and back again would fully restore him.

Fortunately, my recent Maine business had put me in possession of abundant funds, and when I had matured my scheme, and saw that Henry was in tolerable condition to travel, I proposed the trip to him, and he joyfully assented to my plan. I wanted to get him far away, for awhile, from a part of the country which was associated in his mind, more than in mine, with so much misery, and he seemed quite as eager to go. Change of air and scene I knew would do wonders for him bodily, and would build him up again.

We made our preparations and started for the South, going first to Baltimore and then on through the Southern States by railroad to New Orleans. It was late in the fall of 1860, just before the rebellion, when the south was seceding or talking secession, and was already preparing for war. Henry's physical condition compelled us to rest frequently on the way, and we stopped sometimes for two or three days at a time, at nearly every large town or city on the entire route. Everywhere there was a great deal of excitement; meetings were held nearly every night secession was at fever heat, and there was an unbounded expression and manifestation of ill-feeling against the north and against northern men. Nevertheless, I was never in any part of the Union where I was treated with so much courtesy, consideration and genuine kindness as I was there and then. I was going south, simply to benefit the invalid who accompanied me; everybody seemed to know it; and everybody expressed the tenderest sympathy for my son. Wherever we stopped, it seemed as if the people at the hotels, from the landlord to the lowest servant, could not do enough for us. At Atlanta, Augusta, Mobile, and other places, where we made our stay long enough to get a little acquainted, my son and myself were daily taken out to ride, and were shown everything of interest that was to be seen. Henry did not enjoy this journey more than I did-to me as well as to him, the trip was one prolonged pleasure, and by the time we reached New Orleans nearly a month after we left New York, my son had so recuperated that I had every hope of his speedy and full restoration.

It was the beginnings of winter when we reached New Orleans; but during the whole month of December while we remained in that city, winter, if indeed it was winter, which we could hardly believe, was only a prolongation of the last beautiful autumn days we had left at the north. Now Orleans was then at the very height of prosperity; business was brisk, money was plenty, the ships of all nations and countless steamboats from St. Louis, Cincinnati, Louisville and all points up the Mississippi and Ohio rivers lay at the levee. The levee itself, from end to end, for miles along the river front, was one mass of merchandise which had come to the city, or was awaiting shipment. I had never seen a livelier city. Indescribably gay, too, was New Orleans that winter. The city was full of strangers; the hotels were thronged; there were balls every night; the theatres were crowded, and everybody seemed bent on having a good time. With all the rest, there was an extraordinary military furor, and militia companies and regiments paraded the streets every day, while secession meetings were held in various halls, or in the public squares, nearly ever night.

From the St. Charles hotel where we stopped, St. Charles street seemed ablaze and alive all night, and densely thronged all day. Sunday brought no rest, for Sunday, so far as military parades, amusement and general gaiety were concerned, was the liveliest day in the week; and Sunday night the theatres were sure to present their best performances and to draw their largest audiences. And so, from morning till night, and from night till morning again, all was whirl, stir, bustle, business, enjoyment, and excitement. To me, unaccustomed as I was to such scenes, New York even seemed tame and dull, and slow in comparison with New Orleans.

This is a picture of the Crescent City as it presented itself to me and to my son in the early part of the winter before the war. No one knew or even dreamed of the terrible times that were to come. No one believed that war was probable, or even possible; it was well enough, perhaps, to prepare for it; but secession was to be an accomplished fact, and the North and all the world would quietly acknowledge it. This was the general sentiment in the city; though secession, and what would, or what might come of it, was the general topic of talk in the hotels, in the restaurants, at the theatres, in the streets, everywhere. Now and then some southerner with whom I had become acquainted would try to draw me out to ascertain my sentiments on the subject, but I always laughed, and said good naturedly:

"My dear sir, I didn't come down here to talk about secession, but to see if the southern climate would benefit my sick son."

The fact was that I minded my own business, and minded it so well that while I was in New Orleans I managed to find a few patients and sold recipes and medicines enough to pay the entire expenses of our journey thus far, from the North.

Almost every day my son and I drove somewhere up to Carrolton, down to the battle- ground, or on the shell road to Lake Ponchartrain. It was a month of genuine enjoyment to us both; of profit to me pecuniarily; and of the best possible benefit to Henry's health.

Early in January we took passage on one of the finest of the Mississippi steamboats for St. Louis. The boat was crowded, and among the passengers were a good many merchants, Northern men long resident in New Orleans, who thought they saw trouble coming, and accordingly had closed up their business in the Crescent City, and were now going North to stay there. We had on board, too, the usual complement of gamblers and amateur or pro- fessional poker-players, who kept the forward saloon near the bar, and known in the river vernacular as the "Texas" of the boat, lively all day long and well into the night, or rather the next morning. It was ten or eleven days before we reached St. Louis. Nothing notable occurred on the trip; but day after day, as we proceeded northward, and left the soft, sunny south behind us, with the daily increasing coldness and wintry weather, Henry seemed to decline by degrees, and gradually to lose nearly all that he had gained since we left New York. When we reached St. Louis he was seriously sick. I was very sorry we had come away so soon in the season, and proposed that we should return and stay in the south till spring; but Henry would not consent. There was nothing to be done, then, but to hurry on to the east, and when we arrived in New York Henry would not go home to his mother in Unadilla, but insisted upon accompanying me to Boston. I was willing enough that he should go with me, for then I could have him under my exclusive care; but when we arrived in Boston he was so overcome by the excitement of travel, and was so feeble from fatigue as well as disease, that instead of having him go with me to Augusta, as I intended, by the advice of a friend I took him into the country where he could be nursed, be quiet, and be well taken care of till spring. I left him in good hands, promising to come and see him as soon as I could, and the: went back to my old business in Augusta.

It required a little time to knot the new end of that business to the end where I had broken off; three months before; but I was soon in full practice again and was once more making and saving money. I had no matrimonial affair in hand, no temptation in fact, and none but strictly professional engagements to fulfil. In Augusta and in several other towns which I visited, for the whole of the rest of the winter, I was as busy as I could be. Early in the spring I made up my mind to run away for a week or two, and arranged my business so that I could go down into Massachusetts and visit Henry, hoping, if he was better, to bring him back with me to Maine.

Two of my patients in Paris, Maine, had each given me a good horse in payment for my attendance upon them and their families, and for what medicines I had furnished, and I took these horses with me to sell in Boston. I drove them down, putting a good supply of medicines in my wagon to sell in towns on the way, and when I arrived in Boston sold out the establishment, getting one hundred and twenty-five dollars for the wagon, three hundred dollars for one horse, and four hundred dollars for the other-a pretty good profit on my time and medicine for the two patients-and I brought with me besides about eighteen hundred dollars, the net result, above my living expenses, of about three months' business in Maine, and what I had done on the way down through Massachusetts. I am thus minute about this money because it now devolves upon me to show what sort of a family of children my first and worst wife had brought up.

Of these children by my first marriage, my eldest son Henry, since he had grown up, had been with me nearly as much as he had been with his mother, and I loved him as I did my life. Since he became of age, at such times when I was not in prison, or otherwise unavoidably separated from him, we had been associated in business, and had traveled and lived together. I knew all about him; but of the rest of the children I knew next to nothing. Shortly after I sold my horses, one day I was in my room at the hotel, when word was brought to me that some one in the parlor wanted to see me.

I went down and found a young man, about twen- ty-one years of age, who immediately came to me addressing me as "father," and he then presented a young woman, about two years older than he was, as his sister and my daughter. I had not seen this young gentleman since the time when I had carried him off from school and from the farmer to whom he was bound, and had clothed him and taken him with me to Amsterdam and Troy, subsequently sending him to my half-sister at Sidney. The ragged little lad, as I found him, had grown up into a stout, good-looking young man; but I had no difficulty in recognizing him, though I was much at loss to know the precise object of this visit; so after shaking hands with them, and asking then how they were, I next inquired what they wanted?

Well, they had been to see Henry, and he was a great deal better.

I told them I was very glad to hear it, and that I was then on my way to visit him, and hoped to see him in a few days, as soon as I could finish my business in Boston; if Henry was as well as they reported I should bring him away with me.

"But if you are busy here," said my young man, "we can save you both time and trouble. We will go to Henry again and settle his bills for board and other expenses, and will bring him with us to you at this hotel."

This, at the time, really seemed to me a kindly offer; it would enable me to stay in Boston and attend to business I had to do, and Henry would come there with his brother and sister in a day or two. I at once assented to the plan, and taking my well-filled pocket-book from the inside breast pocket of my coat, I counted out two hundred and fifty dollars and gave them to the young man to pay Henry's board, doctor's and other bills, and the necessary car fares for the party. They then left me and started, as I supposed, to go after Henry.

But a few days went on and I saw and heard nothing of Henry. At last word came to me one day that some one down stairs wanted to see me and I told the servant to send him to my room, hoping that it might be Henry. But no; it was my young man, of whom I instantly demanded:

"Where is your brother, whom you were to bring to me a week ago? What have you done with the money I gave you for his bills?"

"I hadn't been near Henry; sister has gone home; and I've spent the money on a spree, every cent of it, here in Boston, and I want more."

"Want more!" I exclaimed in blank amazement:

"Yes, more; and if you don't give it to me, I'll follow you wherever you go, and tell people all I know about you."

"You scoundrel," said I, "you come here and rob, not me, but your poor, sick brother, and then return and attempt to black-mail me. Get out of my sight this instant."

He sprung on me, and made a desperate effort to get my money out of my pocket. We had a terrible struggle. He was younger and stronger than I was, and as I felt that I was growing weaker I called out loudly for help and shouted "Murder!"

The landlord himself came running into the room; I succeeded in tearing myself away, from the grasp of my assailant, and the landlord felled him to the floor with a chair. He then ran to the door and called to a servant to bring a policeman.

"No, don't!" I exclaimed; "Don't arrest the villain, for I can make no complaint against him- he is my son!"

But the landlord was bound to have some satisfaction out of the affair; so he dragged the young man into the hall and kicked him from the top of the stairs to the bottom, where, as soon as he had picked himself up, a convenient servant kicked him out into the street. I have never set eyes on my young man Since his somewhat sudden departure from that hotel.

And when I went to visit my poor Henry a day or two afterwards, I can hardly say that I was surprised, though I was indignant to learn that his brother and sister had never been near him at all since he had been in Massachusetts. They knew where and how he was from his letter's to his mother; they knew, too, from the same letters-for I had notified Henry-at what time I would be in Boston, and with this information they had come on to swindle me. I have no doubt, when the young man came the second time to rob me, he would have murdered me, if the landlord had not come to my assistance. And this was the youngest son of my first and worst wife!!

I found Henry in better condition than I expected, and I took him back with me to Augusta. I did not tell him of his brother's attempt to rob and kill. Me-it would have been too great a shock for him. He stayed with me only a few days and then, complaining of being homesick, he went to visit his mother again.

L. A. Abbot

CHAPTER XV.

A TRUE WIFE AND HOME, AT LAST.

WHERE WERE ALL MY WIVES? - SENSE OF SECURITY - AN IMPRUDENT ACQUAINTANCE - MOVING FROM MAINE - MY PROPERTY IN RENSSELAER COUNTY - HOW I LIVED - SELLING A RECIPE - ABOUT BUYING A CARPET - NINETEEN LAW-SUITS - SUDDEN DEPARTURE FOR THE WEST - A VAGABOND FOR TWO YEARS - LIFE IN CALIFORNIA - RETURN TO THE EAST - DIVORCE FROM MY FIRST WIFE - A GENUINE MARRIAGE - MY FARM - HOME AT LAST.

I remained in Maine nearly two years, hardly ever going out of the State, except occasionally to Boston on business. Making Augusta my residence and head-quarters, I practiced in Portland and in nearly all the towns and cities in the eastern part of the State. During all this time, I behaved myself, in all respects better than I had ever before done in any period of my life. I began to look upon myself as a reformed man; I had learned to let liquor alone, and was consequently in far less, indeed, next to no danger of stepping into the traps in which my feet had been so often caught. I may as well confess it-it was intoxicating liquor, and that mainly, which had led me into my various mad marrying schemes and made me the matrimonial monomaniac and lunatic lover that I was for years. What my folly, my insanity caused me to suffer, these pages have attempted to portray. I had grown older, wiser, and certainly better. I now only devoted myself strictly to my business, and I found profit as well as pleasure in doing it.

What had become of all my wives in the meantime, I scarcely knew and hardly cared. Of course from time to time I had heard more or less about them-at least, a rumor of some sort now and then reached me. About my first and worst wife, at intervals I heard something from Henry, who was still with her, and who frequently wrote to me when he was well enough to do so. Margaret Bradley and Eliza Gurnsey were still carrying on the millinery business in Rutland, and in Montpelier, and were no doubt weaving other and new webs in hopes of catching fresh flies. Mary Gordon, as I learned soon afterwards, was married almost before I had fairly escaped from New Hampshire in my flight to Canada, and she had gone to California with her new husband. Of the Newark widow I knew nothing; but two years of peace, quiet, and freedom from molestation in Maine had made me feel quite secure against any present or future trouble from my past matrimonial misadventures.

I was living in Maine, prudently I think under an assumed name, and as the respectable, and, to my patients and customers, well-known Doctor Blank, I was scarcely liable to be recognized at any time or by any one as the man who had married so many wives, been in so many jails and prisons, and whose exploits had been detailed from time to time in the papers.

Nor, all this while, did I have the slightest fear of detection. I looked upon myself as a victim rather than as a criminal, and for what I had done, and much that I had not done, I had more than paid the penalty. So far as all my business transactions were concerned, my course had always been honorable, and in my profession, for my cures and for my medicines, I enjoyed a good reputation which all my efforts were directed to deserve.

Of course, now and then, I met people in Portland, and especially in Boston, who had known me in former years, and who knew something of my past life; but these were generally my friends who sympathized with my sufferings, or who, at least, were willing to blot out the past in my better behavior of the present. One day in Boston a young man came up to me and said:

How do you do, Doctor?"

"Quite well," I replied; "but you have the advantage of me; I am sure I do not remember you, if I ever knew you."

You don't remember me! Why, I am the son of the jailer in Montpelier with whom you spent so many months before you went to Windsor; I knew you in a minute, and Doctor, I've been in Boston a week and have got 'strapped;' how to get back to Montpelier I don't know, unless you will lend me five or six dollars which I will send back to you the moment I get home."

"I remember you well, now," said I; "you are the little rascal who wouldn't even go and buy me a cigar unless I gave you a dime for doing it; and then, sometimes, you cheated me out of my money; I wouldn't lend you a dollar now if it would save you from six month's imprisonment in your father's filthy jail. Good morning."

And that was the last I saw of him.

I was getting tired of Maine. I had been there longer than I had stayed in any place, except in the Vermont State Prison, for the past fifteen years, and I began to long for fresh scenes and a fresh field for practice. I had accumulated some means, and thought I might take life a little easier-make a home for myself some-where, practicing my profession when I wanted to, and at other times enjoying the leisure I loved and really needed. So I closed up my business in Augusta and Portland, put my money in my pocket, and once more went out into the world on a prospecting tour. My first idea was to go to the far West, and I went to Troy with the intention of staying there a few days, and then bidding farewell to the East forever. The New England States presented no attractions to me; I had exhausted Maine, or rather it had exhausted me; New Hampshire, Vermont, and. Massachusetts had too many unpleasant associations, if indeed they were safe states for me, with my record to live in, and Connecticut I knew very little about. Certainly I had no intention of trying to settle in New Jersey or Pennsylvania. The west was the place; anywhere in the west.

Here was I in Troy, revolving plans in my own mind for migrating to the west, just as Mary Gordon and I had done in the very same hotel, only a few years before; and in the course of a week I came to exactly the same conclusion that Mary and I did- not to go. I heard of a small farm- it was a very small one of only twelve acres-which could be bought in Rensselaer County, not more than sixteen miles from Albany and Troy. I went to see the place, liked it, and bought it for sixteen hundred dollars. There was a small but good house and a barn on the place, and altogether it was a cheap and desirable property. I got a good house-keeper, hired a man, and began to carry on this little farm, raising garden vegetables and fruit mainly, and sending them to market in Albany and Troy. Generally I took my own stuff to market, and sold medicines and recipes as well, and in Albany I had a first rate practice which I went to that city to attend to once or twice a week. While my man was selling vegetables and fruit-I remember I sold a hundred dollars worth of cherries from my farm the first summer- in the market, I was Doctor Blank receiving my patients at Stanwix Hall, or calling upon them at their residences; and when the day's work was over, my man and I rode home in the wagon which had brought us and the garden truck early in the morn- ing. On the whole, this kind of life was exceedingly satisfactory, and I liked it.

I made frequent expeditions to Saratoga and to other places not far from home to attend to cases to which I was called, and to sell medicines; and considering that the main object I had in settling in Rensselaer County was rest and more leisure than I had enjoyed for some years, I had a great deal more to do than I desired. Nevertheless, I might have continued to live on my little farm, raising vegetables, picking cherries, and practicing medicine in the neighborhood, had not the fate, which seemed to insist that I should every little while come before a court of justice for something or other, followed me even here. A certain hardware dealer in Albany, with whom I had become acquainted, proposed to buy one of my recipes, and to go into an extensive manufacture of the medicine. He had read and heard of the fortunes that had been made in patent medicines, by those who understand the business, and he thought he would see if he could not get rich in a year or less in the same way.

After some solicitation I sold him the recipe for one thousand dollars, receiving six hundred dollars down, and a promise of the balance when the first returns from sales of the medicine came in. I also entered into a contract to show the man how to make the medicine, and to give him such advice and assistance in his new business as I could. My hardware friend understood his legitimate business better than he did that which he had undertaken, and although be learned how to manu-facturer the medicine he did not know how to sell it; and after trying it a few weeks, and doing next to nothing, he turned upon me as the author of his misfortunes and sued me for damages.

Incidental to this, and only incidental, is the following: Shortly after I purchased my property, as I was very fond of calling my little farm, in Rensselaer County, I was in Albany one day when it occurred to me that I wanted a carpet for my parlor. I went to the store of a well-known carpet-dealer, and asked to be shown some of his goods. While I was going through the estab-lishment I came across a man who was industriously sewing together the lengths of a cut carpet, and I recognized in him one of my fellow convicts at Windsor. He, however, did not know me, and I doubt if he could have been convinced of my identity as the wretch who plied the broom in the halls of the prison. To him, as he glanced at me, I was only a well-dressed gentleman whom the proprietor was courteously showing through the establishment in the hope of securing a good customer. It was this little circum-stance, I think-my chance meeting with my old fellow-prisoner, and my changed circumstances and appearance which put me beyond recognition by him-that prompted me to the somewhat brazen business that followed:

"I only came in to look to-day," I said to the carpet-dealer; "for the precise sum of money in my pocket at present is eighteen pence, and no more; but if you will cut me off forty yards of that piece of carpeting, and trust me for it, I will pay your bill in a few days, as sure as I live."

My frank statement with regard to my finances seemed to attract the attention of the merchant who laughed and said:

"Well, who are you, anyhow? Where do you live?"

I told him that I was Doctor Blank; that I lived in Rensselaer county on a small place of my own; I raised fruit and vegetables for market; I cured cancers, dropsy, and other diseases when I could; sold medicines readily almost where I would; and was in Albany once or twice a week.

"Measure and cut off the carpet," said he to the clerk who was following us, "and put it in the Doctor's wagon"

The bill was about a hundred dollars, and I drove home with the carpet. It was nearly six weeks afterwards when I went into the store again, and greeted the proprietor. He had seen me but once before and had totally forgotten me. I told him I was Doctor Blank, small farmer and large medical practitioner of Rensselaer County.

"The devil you are! Why, you're the man that bought a carpet of me a few weeks ago; I was wondering what had become of you."

"I'm the man, and I must tell you that the carpet doesn't look well; but never mind-here's a hundred dollars, and I want you to receipt the bill."

"Now," said I, when he returned the bill to me receipted, "the carpet looks firstrate; I never saw a handsomer one in my life."

"Well, you are an odd chap, any how," said the carpet-dealer, laughing, and shaking me by the hand. Almost from that moment we were more than mere acquaintances, we were fast friends. In the course of the long conversation that followed, I told him of my trouble with the hardware man-how I had sold him the recipe; that he had failed, from ignorance to conduct the business properly, and had sued me for damages.

"I know the man," said my new friend; "let him go ahead and sue and be-benefited, if he can; meanwhile, do you keep easy; I'll stand by you."

And stand by me he did through thick and thin. The hardware man sued me no less than nineteen times, and for pretty much everything-damages, debt, breach of contract, and what not. With the assistance of a lawyer whom my friend recommended to me, I beat my opponent in eighteen successive suits; but as fast as one suit was decided he brought another, almost before I could get out of the court room. At last he carried the case to the Supreme Court, and from there it went to a referee. The matter from beginning to end, must have cost him a mint of money; but he went on regardless of the costs which he hoped and expected to get out of me at last.

My long and painful experience, covering many years,

had given me a pretty thorough knowledge of the law's uncertainty, as well as the law's delay, and very early in the course of the present suit, I had quietly disposed of my property in Rensselaer County. I sold the little farm, which cost me sixteen hundred dollars, for twenty-one hundred dollars, and I had had, besides, the profits of nearly two years' farming and a good living from and on the place. I also arranged all my money matters in a manner that I felt assured would be satisfactory to me, if not to my opponent, and then, following the advice of my friend, the carpet-dealer, I let the hardware man sue and be-"benefited if he could." When, however, the case went finally to a referee who was certain, I felt sure, to decide against me, I took no further personal interest in the matter, nor have I ever troubled myself to learn the filial decision. I made up my mind in a moment and decided that the time had come, at last, when it was advisable for me to go to the West.

Westward I went, towards sunset almost, and for the two following years I led, I fear, what would be considered a very vagabond life. I went to Utah, thinking while I was in Salt Lake City, if they only knew my history there I was sure to be elected an apostle, or should be, at any rate, a shining light in Mormondom-only I had taken my wives in regular succession, and had not assembled the throng together. I pushed across the plains, and went to California, remaining a long time in San Francisco. This may have been vagabondism, but it was profitable vagabondism to me. During this long wandering I held no communication with my friends in the East; friends and foes alike had an opportunity to forget me, or if they thought of me they did not know whether I was dead or alive; they certainly never knew, all the time, where I was; and while I was journeying I never once met a man or woman who had been acquainted with me in the past. All the time, too, I had plenty of money; indeed, when, I returned at last I was richer far than I was when I left Albany, and left as the common saying graphically expresses it, "between two days." I had my old resources of recipes, medicines and my profession, and these I used, and had plenty of opportunity to use, to the best advantage. I could have settled in San Francisco for life with the certainty of securing a handsome annual income. I never feared coming to want. If I had lost my money and all other resources had failed, I was not afraid to make a horse-nail or turn a horse-shoe with the best blacksmith in California, and I could have got my living, as I did for many a year, at the forge and anvil.

But I made more money in other and easier ways, and I made friends. In every conceivable way my two years' wandering was of far more benefit to me than I dreamed of when I wildly set out for the West without knowing exactly where, or for what, I was going. The new country, too, had given me, not only a fresh fund of ideas, but a new stock of health -morally and physically I was in better condition than I ever was before in my life. I had a clear head; a keen sense of my past follies; a vivid consciousness of the conse-quences which such follies, crimes they may be called, are almost certain to bring. I flattered myself that I was not only a reformed prisoner, but a reformed drunkard, and a thoroughly restored matrimonial monomaniac.

And when I returned, at last, to the East, and went once more to visit my near and dear friends in Ontario County, I was received as one who had come back from the dead. When I had been here a few weeks, and had communicated to my cousins so much of the story of my life as I then thought advisable, I took good counsel and finally did what I ought to have done long years before. I commenced proper legal proceedings for a divorce from my first and worst wife. I do not need to dwell upon the particulars; it is enough to say, that the woman, who was then living, so far from opposing me, aided me all she could, even making affidavit to her adultery with the hotel clerk at Bainbridge, long ago, and I easily secured my full and complete divorce. Now I was, indeed, a free man-all the other wives whom I had married, or who had married me, whether I would or no, were as nothing; some were dead and others were again married. It may be that this new, and to me strange sense of freedom, legitimate freedom, set me to thinking that I might now secure a genuine and true wife, who would make a new home happy to me as long as we both should live.

Fortune, not fate now, followed me, led me rather and guided my footsteps. It was not many months before I met a woman who seemed to me in every way calculated to fill the first place in that home which I had pictured as a final rest after all my woes and wanderings. From mutual esteem our acquaintance soon ripened into mutual love. She was all that my heart could desire. I was tolerably well off; my position was reputable; my connections were respectable. To us, and to our friends, the match seemed a most desirable one. It was no hasty courtship; we knew each other for months and learned to know each other well; and with true love for each other, we had for each other a genuine respect. I frankly told her the whole story of my life as I have now written it. She only pitied my misfortunes, pardoned my errors, and, one bright, golden, happy autumn day, we were married.

In the northeastern part of the State of New York on the banks of a broad and beautiful river, spread out far and near the fertile acres of one of the finest farms in the country. It is well stocked and well tilled. The surrounding country is charming -game in the woods, and fish in the streams afford abundant sport, and the region is far away from large cities, and remote even from railroads. I do not know of a more delightful place in the whole world to live in. On the farm I speak of, a cottage roof covers a peaceful, happy family, where content and comfort always seem to reign supreme. A noble woman, a most worthy wife is mistress of that house; joyous children move and play a among the trees that shade the lawns; and the head of the household, the father of the family, is the happiest of thee group.

That farm, that family, that cottage, that wife, that happy home are mine-all mine. I have found a true wife and a real home at last.

My story is told; and if it should suggest to the reader the moral which is too obvious to need rehearsal, one object I had in telling the story will have been accomplished.

www.ingramcontent.com/pod-product-compliance
Lightning Source LLC
Chambersburg PA
CBHW032002040426
42448CB00006B/462